OH YEAH

OH YEAH
A BEAR POETRY ANTHOLOGY

**RAYMOND LUCZAK,
EDITOR**

B

Bearskin Lodge Press
Syracuse, NY

In Gratitude

The editor is grateful to Eric Thomas Norris and Tom Steele for their editorial input. He is also deeply indebted to Les K. Wright for enabling this anthology to happen.

Reprints

Jer Loudenback's "Gingers" was translated from ASL into English by Raymond Luczak.
Raymond Luczak's "The Embrace" first appeared in *Impossible Archetype*.
Ed Madden's "My Husband Who is Not My Husband" first appeared in his book *A pooka in Arkansas* (Word Works, 2023).
Daniel Edward Moore's "Remember How Good It Feels to Be Good to Yourself" first appeared in *The Flint Hills Review*; "Light's Toxic Hymn of Pleasure," *Impossible Archetype*.
Mark Ward's "Heft" first appeared in *Burly Tales: Fairy Tales for the Hirsute and Hefty Gay Man* (Steve Berman, ed.; Lethe Press).

for
Mark Ward

CONTENTS

CONTENTS

CONTENTS

Oh Yeah: Some Thoughts on Bears and Poetry
by Raymond Luczak

Bears and poetry should not even exist together. Bears often evoke a blue-collar vibe with their T-shirts, baseball caps, and jeans when they hang out in bars. Sometimes they show off the results of lifting weights at the gym; sometimes their bellies droop.

And poetry? Such obtuse pronouncements seem immaterial to the way we live today. Yet poets are often the ones to express inarticulated gasps of feeling so sharply that we feel a flash of recognition, an acknowledgment of our own experiences, while reading their work: *Oh yeah.*

Even though I had been thin all my life, I was often made to feel that when I came out in the mid-1980s, I wasn't muscular enough, fashionably coiffed, or smooth enough. I was overly hairy, which I didn't like much because too many guys complained about my fur once we got naked together. Some brought up the idea of waxing my back a few times; even one stipulated that as a requisite for our relationship.

These one-night stands taught me how to hate my own body. My self-image, which was already low, sank even further. I lost whatever self-confidence I might've had whenever I saw an attractive man. I did not believe that I could be sexy enough for him. I didn't dare to ask anyone out on dates. Who'd want a hairy Deaf guy anyway?

The first time I happened to see a copy of *BEAR Magazine* in the back of A Different Light Bookstore in New York City was absolutely galvanizing. *Look at me,* the chunky and furry men who took it all off for the camera said. *This is the body that nobody wanted while I was coming out.* Such self-acceptance had made them far hotter than any model who'd been groomed to physical perfection.

Suddenly I felt a bit better about my own body. *Oh yeah.*

Even though the study of poetry seems to have been largely relegated to the dustbin, it remains a vital art. Why else do so many people still write poems? There's very little—if any—money in the "po biz." Even the most famous poets living today don't get much ink in the mainstream media. Which is a shame, because great poetry, like great film scripts, often demands a succinctness of expression sorely lacking these days.

INTRODUCTION

Poetry still matters because we want our experiences—if not our perspectives on the past as well as the world changing around us—to mean *something,* all the while flexing our own limber muscles of language.

Yet we gay readers are selfish at heart. Feeling lonely and misunderstood at times, we're constantly seeking to affirm the core elements of our own experiences through the words of strangers whose names are on the cover. Like Tennessee Williams so unforgettably said at the end of his play *A Streetcar Named Desire,* "Whoever you are—I have always depended on the kindness of strangers."

Gay poets seem most like those mysterious strangers we see sitting on the train, their thoughts aswirl with lust and heartache, and looking out the window late at night with an occasional glance back at us. *Oh yeah.*

Times have truly changed since the mid-1990s when I first spotted *BEAR Magazine.* Actually, "changed" is the wrong verb; "accelerated" is more like it. The power of porn magazine editors to define—and, through their choice of models, dictate—what constituted male physical beauty has long ago dissipated. Erotic selfies shot by men who are clearly not gym bunnies are shared with abandon. Middle-aged men have joined in the act. In fact, some of them offer even more intimate visuals through pay sites. And they don't always sport large erections!

However, what's been largely missing amidst such erotic diversions are the conversations we need to have with each other as gay men. Sometimes I feel we've become so pornified that we've forgotten to see each other as *human beings* with very complicated feelings about their own bodies. Many of us don't even feel comfortable in the bodies that we're given.

This anthology is an attempt to remind ourselves that we need to do better about accepting ourselves *as we are* and one another *as they are.* We need to remember that when Bears initially connected as a community, it was actually a communal attempt at body positivity. To want someone who's overweight, for instance, and to be *open* about that desire without shame, was very much a political act, a statement of resistance against societal expectations of physical beauty. It still is today.

Regardless of their weight and size and identity within the Bear community, the poets in this anthology have much to demonstrate how we're not so alone after all. It's my hope that reading their work in these pages, you'll catch yourself nodding and going: *OH YEAH.*

THE POETS

Two Jacks in the Bear's Lair
The Titanic Seventies before the Iceberg of AIDS
(An Epic Narrative Poem of Body Invention)

Under the Stars of Ursa Major,
it was a brilliant San Francisco season
sun-drenched with drought and sweat
men everywhere on this peninsula of men
that Bicentennial Summer of '76
before the Titanic Seventies party cruised
innocent into the iceberg of AIDS
us sitting together at his kitchen table
my first visit in his handsome bear lair
tall garden-windows, six French doors
in pairs winged open, floor to ceiling,
framing the Sunday afternoon golden hour
of Vermeer light, yellow smoke yellow fog
sliding drifting across the waters of the East Bay.

I have known such virile afternoons
lingering in chambers by the sea.
Tankers down from the Alaska Pipeline
crewed by hairy roustabouts
floating at anchor motionless below us
with builder-grade roughnecks on board
far out against the widescreen horizon
spread out against the skyline with
the smoke from his cigar
bluing blurring the view,
his hiking boots kicked up on his coffee table,
trousers rolled, his big back curved deep,
settling a pillow into the slouch
of his wicker chair.

He inhaled his Oliva Robusto and
gave me face, smiling through his beard
smoking and toking cigar and joint

taking two hits of the Castro Blitz
he grew in his kitchen garden
that summer when we and everyone
and everything were all so new
to the city the world the universe
almost so good it was unthinkable
to ask the overwhelming question:
How long can this joy last?
His grass lifted us twin namesakes.
"Jack," he toasted *basso*,
over longnecks of beer.
"Jack," I toasted *profundo*.
"Here's to full moons on dark nights."
We laughed joke-toasting our pet beards,
the easiest thing men have to morph
imperfect shapes of face head and look
adding jaw and chin and cheek bones
masking acne scars and sunfried wrinkles
trading hits on the joint
whorls of smoke rubbing
against the windowpanes,
music coming from another room.

His turntable spinning
love songs of county rock,
the Eagles thrumming
thirty-three-and-a-third revolutions per minute
mermen singing each to each
the soundtrack of our rainbow revolution,
new kids in town, life in the fast lane,
the long the lean the mass the muscle
the short the fat the brown the black
sex immigrants escaping suicide
in hometowns of body shaming
playground mean girls and bully boys
assault weapon straight mouths and fists
killer bears and closet brutes
perversely hot

red-meat red-state rednecks,
neighborhood chunks
of locally-sourced Neanderthals,
village idiots bragging
I've lived here all my life
because I'm a moron,
so don't let the sun set on you, faggot,
rowdy punks with their own redneck gaydar
search parties attacking our bodies
our gay body language
hooting hollering spewing the toxic waste
of their Pentecostal inhuman voices
waking us to drown us
shaming our bodies
making Yoo-Hoo Cooee Faggot flaws
out of our natural gifts never straight enough,
depressing us, causing us
to flee our homes
escaping the pale of their inbred gangs
validating our queer bodies with new ways
of freeing seeing being our bodies our selves
in gay sanctuary cities.

Welcome to the Hotel California
where you can check in to San Francisco,
but you can never leave
and why would you want to?

We walked shirtless through
his House of Hibernation,
meticulous, the E-ticket tour,
opening doors to rooms,
talking, smoking, eating peaches,
explaining his brother Esau was a hairy man,
kissing necking nibbling nippling
rubbing sperm-spackled fur of bellies,
him thinking after a stoned bear hug
of another nook, another cranny,

another room, downstairs, a playroom, a den.
(Was it time to turn back,
or descend the stairs for sex?)
A bear's house is his body and
he was house-proud sharing his burly privacy
the way a stripling teen
in a highschool locker room
first dares show off
his amazing new changeling body
sprouting first fur as his inner bear
grows out of his smooth boycub skin
in his Spring Awakening.

We sat together, him a Jack, me a Jack,
a pair of Jacks in a world of Jokers
and Queens and Douches wild,
two men from the clan of the cave bear
dealing poker hands in the full house Jack built,
trading stories of homes, prices, interest,
of gays moving into neighborhoods,
claiming territory, the geography of our bodies,
good yet that summer, good enough,
both thirty-seven, facing forty,
not our fathers' straight forty,
the new gay forty: thirty.

Squeezing the universe into a fistful of sex,
bears sacred to Odin, the God of Berserkers,
we made ritual of the afternoon harmony,
stoned satisfied silent, teasing, tripping
on the afternoon hanging over the Bay,
watching a white cruise ship
caught in a gauze of haze,
navigated to port by an escort of tugboats,
crews of horny hirsute able seamen,
hairballing deck hands and stewards
itching to hit the city, new tits in town
with thoughts of 24-hour shore leave

lusting for Castro bars Folsom baths
Tenderloin gloryholes
the Embarcadero YMCA
ship pennants waving flags fluttering,
under the X-braced trestles of the Bay Bridge,
top-deck radar inching tight
passing under gray girders,
we two born bears watching
rubbing and tugging
our genes in our own rub-a-dub tub
our handkerchief flags of yellow and red flying
skimming under the trestle bridge of forty,
still cool yet, hale yet, hearty yet,
inventing our bearish futures,
hirsute sex the bonding between us.

In his rooms where chasers come and go
talking of Michael and Angelo,
we asked what is it about bodies
and fur and muscles and health,
vitamins and minerals, poppers
and Quaaludes and ether,
drugs spread out upon a table
by dealers of insidious intent peddling
magic mushrooms and acid and
steroid stacks of Dianabol to build bulk
over margaritas in sawdust restaurants
with oysters on the half shell
in fern bars on Polkstrasse
in leather bars on Folsom
in clone bars on Castro
where come Saturday night
without pecs you're dead.

If life ever fucks him over,
deals him a bad hand, a sick Old Bear,
he wants marmalade tea and cakes and ices
and intravenous vitamin C every hour.

In his office, on his desk, we flopped open
the *Physicians Big Book of Drug Reference*,
asking the overwhelming question,
so stoned that Sunday on his organic Blitz
searching the index, looking up steroids,
the wild card, the most secret
most transfiguring
most used drug on Castro,
seeking a loophole for a risky roll of the dice.
Do we dare?
Do we dare lay a bet to bulk and buff
born baby-bear bodies of boyhood
(a tiny month's tiny dose of body positivity)
for transformative musclebear glory?
Despite lickety-lickety gossip
of side-effects and impotence
and weeping and prayers
and blue balls from little blue pills,
heart cries of boyhood dysmorphia
caused by scrums of boys playing ball sports
cries escaping full-throated from slender
youngyoungyoung Castronaut cubs
in 28x30 Levi's, red hankies right,
in search of physiques and avoirdupois
feeling how their arms and legs are thin,
too thin for Saturday night fever.

What a comedy of Ursus Erectus.
Two Jacks shuffling cards of medical advice
like Adam and Eve a bit obtuse
in a Paradise casino
making decisions for radical revisions.
Do we dare eat just one itty bitty bite
of Eden's magic steroid that will turn us
Bear Spirit animals godlike?

His handsome features frowning fair,
his burly arms laid along the table,

downed with thick brown hair,
he emerged from the cumulus of his cigar,
amused, smiling at our conversation,
his blond moustache ticking to gray.
Do I dare presume tell/remind him/me
how his/my head of hair is growing thin
as mortal bodies betray us
who may be nothing more
than a pair of ragged bear claws
scuttling across the floors of silent seas.

Talking dirty while we stroked,
I confessed my lechery for voyeur fuckerie
with men in authority fluid with sperm,
eye-balling a California Highway Patrol
motorcycle cop walking
with Command Presence
into lunch in my office cafeteria
golden helmet tucked like a football
under the crook of his big arm,
noticing everything,
never noticing me sitting near him,
my necktie asserted by a simple pin,
me from my desk chair, him from his motorcycle,
sitting at right angles to him wearing
his blue-and-gold CHP shoulder patch
embroidered with a grizzly bear.
Good God! I'd be his tool, deferential,
glad to be of use, peering at him
over the perfect gay hunter's blind
of my newspaper "Sporting Green"
gay-gazing into him,
memorizing his moustache,
five-o'clock shadow visible at high noon,
badge, tan shirt, short sleeves, big biceps,
sky-blue tie, gun belt,
bike breeches striped blue and gold
tucked into lickable black-leather riding boots,

the camera in my head recording
virility vérité fuck films
of testosterone worship saluting him
eating two burgers two tables away,
flexing my thighs in a zipless fuck,
cumming quietly, a silent scream in my suit pants
a trick stealth hands taught me young
how to cum being slow jerked in the third row
of a crowded movie theater.

With Jack, our Bear Cult story,
twenty million years
after the first bear appeared on earth,
started months before this blue Sunday afternoon
cruising each other's fur upholstery,
stalking the strength of stature
among the hottest hottest in the heat
of the Barracks bath roughhouse, 2 AM,
another gorgeous restless night
in a gorgeous cheap hotel,
my Saturday night ending meeting
his Sunday morning beginning,
coming face to face with his fresh attitude
(Let us go then, you and I)
that in my Barracks room, number 336
(first left at the top of the stairs)
got slapped back and forth frolicking
in mutuality between us,
a courtship of bears, beasts,
idealists under the acid-red light,
bear shadows flicker-fucking
on the wall of Plato's cave.
(There is more to reality than senses grasp.)
Neither kneeling,
rearing up roaring up on hind legs
beard to beard sportfucking,
primal in a black room,
a chivalry of sex with the proper stranger

jacking off in mutual raging satisfaction
of homomasculine respect
wondering if repetition domesticates
growling tricks into husbears.
(Is it impossible to say just what I mean?)

That summer of sunny weekend afternoons
we two of a kind, with other pals, attendant lords,
foundational bears in our sleuth of bears
redolent musky odor of bear sperm,
standing shirtless in jeans sunning
in the habitat of Castro Street
where every bear that ever there was
was gathered there because, because,
a hug of rainbow bears
black brown red yellow polar and panda
butts and backs rubbing scratching up against
the white wood windowsill of Donuts & Things,
a Teddy Bear Picnic of Daddy bears
hungry for chicken marinated in bear grease
scouting new cubs recruiting chasers
licking cubs clean
measuring our lives with coffee cups to go,
watching the madding crowd
the festive sidewalk pride parade
containing multitudes
of lions and tigers and bears
at the corner of gay vanity fair,
card sharps playing 52-Pickup at
the ground zero of 18th Street and Castro,
thousands of incoming gay refugees
one of every kind,
labeled abled mislabled disabled fabled,
legends before they became history
half of Noah's ark,
sorting each other
under the tall blade sign
of the Castro Theater marquee.

We have known them all, those men,
as if hundreds would be enough
when thousands were never enough,
known the eyes of faces we'd meet,
crowds hanging out
passing time in mass foreplay
years and years
of Saturday and Sunday afternoons
before the nights of bars and baths,
cheering lovely shirtless men
young enough to think they'll live forever,
leaning out open windows
of their third-floor flats
blasting disco on stereos into the intersection,
with nude men with speed-lean bodies
fan dancing for joy on rooftops
waving the Bear Flag of Free California
above cafes and shops and bookstores
where seven naked sun bears
acrobats in combat boots and jockstraps,
hairy butts furry backs tits and taints ahoy
mooning the swooning crowd,
climbing into position
up a fire-escape ladder, three stories up,
a sex circus act,
a daisy chain of dancing bears
each one being rimmed carnivorous for ass
rimming the butt on the rung above
to cheers from the intoxicating street party,
sex immigrants sweating out
old viral toxins of hometowns,
sex refugees celebrating the good luck
of finding and fucking so many
polymorphous versions and perversions
of gay bodies, cubs chubs otters transbruins,
bar-hopping in the girth and mirth
of a pub crawl
Midnight Sun to Badlands to Toad Hall

to Moby Dick to Lion Pub to Bear Hollow,
sizing up baskets, faces, bodies, minds,
comparing sexcapades over brunch plates
of Bears Benedict $2.22 with smoked salmon
at the Castro Café and the Norse Cove,
trading tall tales of tricks
the divine decadence of the decade,
raconteurs of our own lives,
character actors of our own devise,
and finally old billy bruins, curmudgeons
who prayed our lives would continue
like long days of heaven
like this languorous golden afternoon
hanging out happy in his kitchen
over tankers floating motionless,
hung out of all perspective
on the flat face of the East Bay.

What is it? This visit? This mancave?
A Sunday afternoon Vespers?
A communion of cocksuckers?
A taking of toast and tea,
Oolong, imported?
I'm old. I'm old.
I've seen this moment flicker,
a memory, again and again.
A pair of twentieth-century Jacks
kicked back like lords in a house of cards
threatened in a mondo disturbo universe
wondering out loud,
and re-wondering,
how long shit as fabulous as this could last
because nothing this good can last forever,
knowing our quickening golden hour
to be too soon our past,
knowing our past
will be a strange country to new boys
hairy cubs and hairless chasers

who will not likely sing each to each
of us because we did things differently,
and they won't care
about the Golden Age
of our flickering moment of greatness
because no one really wants
lectures from Lazarus
back from the cave of the dead.

Every pair of Jacks in a paradox of Paradise
knows when to hold 'em, fold 'em, and walk away.
Old gamblers know every hand's a winner
till it's gone with the wind.
So I kiss Jack goodbye.

Yet maybe seven young smart bears
escaping bear traps,
seven Stars of the Constellation Ursa Major,
in a meme of Four of a Kind
plus a Pair of new Jacks
plus a Wild One
calling our bets, cubs yet unborn
accepting shaping celebrating
the born bodies dealt them
will stand grave vigil
gay gazing at the taxidermy
of our grizzled bodies on exhibit
vintage bears
in permanent hibernation under glass
at the Gay Unnatural History Museum
in our Gay Nostalgia District.
11 to 4 PM Daily
Closed Mondays and Holidays
Adults, $4, Seniors $2, Youth Free
Those retro lads
weeping laughing jerking conjuring
with the magical thinking of masturbation
fantasies of a time-travel return

to the lost Eden
of the auld lang syne
of our emancipating first decade
after Stonewall
when pioneer bears
making alt-bodies okay
came out to play tennis
before the ultimate
body dysphoria of AIDS
threatened our species with extinction
we acted up against.

JOHN GENEST

Just Right?

Once upon a time, there were three bachelor Bears
who lived in a house of their own.
The first Bear was Big, the second Middle-Sized,
and the third was Little; this is known.

They went out for a stroll so their porridge could cool
but returned to find chaos instead.
Little's bowl was emptied and his chair had been broke
by a golden-haired miss in his bed!

She awoke with a start and leapt up to depart
and jumped out of the window to flee,
leaving behind three Bears with a chair to repair
and some porridge shared in harmony.

As I ponder the morale of this hairy tale,
I find it disappointing to see
that the narrowing favor of that blond home invader
can now be found in our hairstory.

I seem to recall the Bears starting it all
as a counter to gay status quo.
For those big guys with hair, there was finally somewhere
that they and their admirers could go.

Spread on magazine pages, they became all the rage
and there's personal ads in the back!
If you're ready to blow, pop in a video
to watch them suck and fuck as you jack.

Bearphernalia galore, shop at our online store
as you learn new vocubulary.
If you think you're the best, compete in a contest
and aspire to Bear royalty.

At a Bear night or run, get together, have fun,
do a shot or some drugs, buy a round.
Get on up and dance, too; when the music is through,
can you guys hear that strange clique-ing sound?

Otter, wolf, bear or cub, you're all part of the club
if you've won genetic lottery.
But for those who did not, you can still cast your lot
in the hopes you might see and be seen.

And it's here we begin to see a new spin
on the morale of our ursine fable
that some Bears have now spoken, your chair remains broken,
there's no room for you at their table.

"You're too skinny, too fat; you're too this and not that,
you're too old or too young; you're not hairy.
Not the right color fur, lacking musculature,"
they might say; criticisms will vary.

For too hot can turn cold and too hard is the mold
into which some expect us to fit.
You can try to do so or jump out the window
and just follow your bliss till you find it.

Bear's an identity and a community;
you can embrace them both and that's cool.
You should not have to fight to fit in as "just right"
so less Goldilocks, more Golden Rule.

JOHN GENEST

Love in the Time of COVID

An old friend of mine posted he had caught COVID;
"Beware the ides of March," the Bard said.
He was one of the first and that post was his last;
three weeks later, I learned he was dead.

When shutdowns and masks drove us all to stay home
my workplace was now by my bed,
commuting by Zoom and losing with Noom
and living inside my own head.

The next year, we stepped a toe back in the world
with vaccines created and restrictions laxed
to gather together, but six feet apart
as if after our exile such distance could last.

I reached out in Bear apps as I had all that time
and kept checking my traps to see what I might find
and you reached back to me from not so far at all
and we met Mischief Night and we both had a ball.

In the new year, we grew even closer together,
met each other's folks and it kept getting better.
You moved in with me lock, stock and Xbox by June
and by fall you were training to do something new.

But that Mischief Night, *déjà vu* came into play
as you brought us home COVID along with your pay.
We weathered it better than had my old friend,
but again it portended the start of our end.

You weren't feeling sexual once it had passed
but you'd work on it; so I believed.
After false starts and bait and switch, drunken attempts,
I should have just told you to leave.

You had asked me then too if it's okay to quit;
the new job was too hard and you weren't feeling it.
I gave my permission, became our breadwinner,
not knowing this was just the start of your grift.

When the ides of March came in the following year,
you finally found part-time work.
You played with your Xbox and self every night
and then slept as I worked and I jerked.

I drove you to Driver's Ed, footed our bills
and supported you in mental health.
You got back two grand from your taxes that spring
and you spent every cent on yourself.

I felt more tricked than treated the next Mischief Night,
when my intuition finally kicked in.
I made you admit that you no longer loved me
as all that year you hadn't been.

And later that week after you were ejected,
I turned on my cell phone to read
that again you had COVID and I should get tested;
a parting gift I didn't need.

JOHN GENEST

My Life in Reverse

A decade has passed since I looked in the mirror
reflecting on what I saw there.
I've become the Daddybear that I predicted
but of other things, not so aware.

It began a few years back walking through campus,
a sudden pain in my right knee.
A meniscal tear that came out of nowhere
marked the start of this Bear's atrophy.

I was using a cane just to counter the pain
and it helped me to carry along
but as my joints compressed, both my legs felt more stressed
till I had diagnosed what was wrong.

I used to walk miles every morning and night
and worked out on machines at the gym,
but I'm wheeling around in a rollator now
after osteoarthritis set in.

I'll need to lose weight to have both knees replaced,
something I will struggle to achieve.
I've had steroids and gel both injected as well
in the hopes they'd provide some relief.

So I do my best now to keep zipping around
as I roll myself backwards down halls.
I've become rather good at reverse rollerhood
and I've only had three or four falls.

But I miss glory days when I used to go graze
at porn theaters, booths, and the baths.
Some guys don't want to screw when you're R2-D2,
and in spite of this, I have to laugh.

I put right on the table that I am disabled
when chasers read through my profile.
If they think this is wrong, they can just move along
'cause it wouldn't be worth both our while.

I'm a Grizzly in bed, love to give and get head,
get my ass plowed like a quarterback's huddle,
and once you shoot your load like creampie à la mode,
I'm a Teddy Bear ready to cuddle.

Love to deep-kiss with you and some pillow talk too;
I'm your big spoon if you need a nap.
If you're spending the night, could you turn off that light?
I hope you don't mind my C-PAP.

I will shower with you once our breakfast is through
and I'll hope that you have a great day.
I can be all these things, but I'm just wondering
where that Bear is who's willing to stay.

So I'll wait for the sequel and search for my equal
as hope springs eternal for me
for although I'm disabled, I'm as loving and stable
as a Daddy could possibly be.

Here in the Nutmeg State, I hope it's not too late
for this Yogi to find his Boo Boo.
I'm ambitious and strong; I just can't stand for long
and I hope that won't matter to you.

BENJAMIN S. GROSSBERG

Preparing for a First Date at Fifty

A razor scraped along the side of the neck
and salt-and-pepper years drop

in clumps of shaving cream. Next scissors
to the beard: from hobo to Hasid

to homo in a burst of cuts. And a tar
facial scrub for red blotches: your head

is a fruit, and these indicate the lee side
of ripe, a use-now sag that will soon

go to rot. Then shower, the water hot.
Dressing is strategic. You, the general

of a great power bled dry by the last
few wars, shift meager resources around

the globe, hoping no one realizes.
Tight holds things in. Loose obscures.

Both raise troubling questions.
Your date, too, is fifty. Has he learned

a little forbearance? At this age, first dates
sprinkle sporadically across the calendar

like Friday the 13ths, but with at least
the possibility of better luck.

The doorbell rings. You open to a man
you haven't yet met in person. Red hair,

very little of it, blue eyes, wrinkles,
and three days growth of beard more

gray than gold. Are you pleased?
He looks old enough to be your father

as you still think of your father, not like
the eighty-year-old your father is now.

BENJAMIN S. GROSSBERG

The Company of Men

1.

Four, five hours afterwards, you are awake. You have slept intermittently, your eyes suddenly opening, fully alert.

2.

You wonder if he had done coke in the bathroom right as you texted him that you'd arrived, and if you had taken some of it in, the exhalation of it, though he kept his lips, his face turned away. If, eight hours later, a drug was revving your brain like a dog's lead wound again and again around a palm, finally choking the animal back. Coke or meth.

3.

Best just to let the man talk, to create conditions where he can. On his bed, on his back, raised on his elbows so he can look at you. Best to let him tell you he was married to a woman for seven years. To a woman, yeah. Bitching all the time, he says. Let him call her a coke whore. Say she put on seventy pounds. And be with me? Nod as you look at him. Maybe I'm vain, I don't know, he says. But seventy pounds and be with me?

4.

His face: roiled, twitchy. Let him tell you he has been up three days. React honestly: you serious? Three days? Since Thursday, he says. And didn't he text you he was tired? Off work, he'd texted. Just come to my place. You like me and I like you, right? Just come to my place.

5.

He makes a show of putting his cellphone under his clothes, so you will know he isn't filming. I don't do that shit, he says, sliding his phone underneath. A lot of guys do that shit.

6.

He says he did them himself. Some guy drew them for him, but he did them himself. Single needle. Fantastically detailed. How about the one on your back? That's Thor with a raven. He turns over, stretching out as he's talking. Can you see the raven? With your forefinger, trace Thor, who stretches, warm and soft, from blade to blade. Behind Thor in the same dark blue, Nordic mountains rising.

7.

With the palm of your hand, firmly cuff the back of his neck, applying a little pressure, like how a mother cat carries a kitten, placing her mouth there, the forepaws limp in front of her. This gesture, this cuffing, is one way a man can—at a distance, with an outstretched arm—hold another. Though you are both on his bed when you do it.

8.

White supremacist tattoos. He will point this out. Let him tell you he doesn't believe in that shit, and, well, yeah, he likes to be with his kind, who doesn't? Say it must have been scary, being inside. That's something you can say honestly. I can handle myself, he says. Though he can't see your face, nod again.

9.

You want to do this. And/or there is no other safe way to leave.

10.

Afterward, don't say you are leaving, even as you begin the motions of leaving. Shirt, jeans, socks, jacket, keys. Don't say goodbye, even as you move to the door.

Notes from a PrEP Diary / One More Month

It's what I said last month. It wouldn't be easy
to give up: this Kevlar, this diamond S
across my chest, the fantasy
of ripping open a button-down, to reveal it there.
Last week, Phil and I walked this suburban neighborhood,
and he said, much too loudly, that he didn't know why
he was taking it anymore since he never gets laid—
that was the term he used—and I glanced around to see
my neighbors' windows open
and wondered which part I found worrying,
the phrase "getting laid" or the unapologetic
gayness of it all: on hardly passionate Roberts Lane.
And finally decided neither was so bad but still
gestured with my hand, a lowering motion.
We still don't know, Phil said more quietly, what this stuff
does to our bodies, not years of it.
Phil wants to marry again.
He was married in all but name for twenty years
until marriage was legalized. Then his husband ran off
and married somebody else. Phil visits me
for an afternoon, for a test drive.
Think double bind. He knows—we do—
many of the things one can have now
are mutually exclusive. We can have PrEP
and its freedoms; that is to say
we can poison our bodies in order to more fully possess them:
what they can do and what bonds
that doing can, sometimes, create.
But the pill creates expectations, too—
a shuffling through men, even if to find that bond,
but so quickly, perhaps, as to foreclose its possibility.
Can a man form connection another way?
Other than sex, when do men let themselves be known?
Or, of course, we can *not* take PrEP
and have a physical reluctance that is, of necessity,

an emotional reluctance. Or to put it another way:
Phil and I know that men can get fucked into love,
but if there's another method, we haven't seen it.
Which is why he hasn't given up the pill.
And me, walking side-by-side with him
knowing the freedoms he and I could pursue
together, why haven't I given it up?
At the right volume, it's good to spend time with Phil,
though I hesitate, perhaps we both do, on the edge
of possibility: *no,* we think, *not quite, not quite good enough.*

ALEX CARRIGAN

Ruminations at the Red Bear Brewing Company

As I sit at the bar, digging my
elbows into the rough countertop,
I have to wonder if I'm bear enough
for anyone here tonight.

My beard is the result of
neglecting to shave for weeks,
as wild, unkempt, and itchy
as a field of briars.

I have a belly I've been steadily
growing since childhood, with
stretch marks that remind me
I'll never be a mother bear.

I don't know how desirable
I truly am at gay bars
(or straight bars for that matter,
which I rarely go to despite
being bisexual).

I like to believe that I can
easily slip into a bear skin
like the boyfriend from *Midsommar*.
I have the raw materials, but
is that truly enough to be one?

Maybe I just need to invest in
leather harnesses or vests.
Maybe I need the nerve to be
shirtless in public.
Or maybe I need a round-trip
ticket to Folsom to finally feel
like I'm truly a bear.

I don't think anyone will
confirm that for me tonight.
Everyone's eyes are fixed on the
drag show that's playing out before us,
No one will notice me sitting here
nursing my stout beer while
catsuits and corsets are paraded around.

I'll finish my drink as I hand the
queen a dollar and hope that the
next time I come here, that someone
will admire my bearness and let me
put my paws on them in return.

Then I could finally confirm
that all the times I was mocked
for being fat, for being slightly femme,
for having long hair for a boy
would all be worth it once
I met that one person who
would bother with a bear like me.

A cute girl getting drinks for her
table did compliment my manbun
before she walked away,
so maybe I'm not too far off
from that day.

ALEX CARRIGAN

A Bear of the DMV Area
a cento of text from the DC Gaybros Discord group

Is there a homosexual gathering for NYE
that an average bear can go to?
I am hairy and I don't
trim or shave.

I just don't want to be
the only bear on the floor.
I feel like Uproar is the bar for
bigger, hairy guys, given that it's a bear bar.
It has a really cool vibe too.

But then the twinks found out there's
free food at Bear Happy Hour.
I'll start my own bear colony,
open to all those who leave
the body shaming at the door.

I do like to get the chasers to bear events I am at.
When bears are into me, they get
nervous and run away.
Every time I try a bear smirk,
it just looks like I'm having a light stroke.
I, too, am full of anxiety bees with a smidge
of depression bears. Just let me be
a switch bear guy and leave it at that.

One of the little things about dating bears is
checking to see if that little bottle in
his bathroom is bear oil or poppers.
I pity the bear whose monster dick
makes you gag. Haha, I'm pretty open
to anything, honestly.
I wanna see bears on ice!!!

Kuma-kei

I don't want to
be a man in a
manga by Gengoroh Tagame.

I don't want to be tied
up with ropes like
a Thanksgiving turkey,
but I do want a body that's
emphasized by lines and forms.

I don't want to be gagged
and forced to my knees,
but I want my breath taken away
and to find a new faith to
prostrate myself before.

I don't want to be stepped
on, but I do want to admire
the steps of the person
who walks alongside me.

I don't want to have my
body shaped and molded
by someone else's predilections,
but I do want my shape and mold
to match someone's husband material.

I don't want my ecstasy to
become public spectacle, but
I do want it to be something
genuine when I do show
it to someone else.

I want my face to
be as sharp as a line drawing.

I want my body hair to lay
softly across my chest
like a barley field.

I want pride and passion
in my body that could
break any chains or ropes
like a bundle of chopsticks
across my knee.

I don't want to be
a man *in* a Gengoroh Tagame
manga, but I do want
to be a man *from* a
Gengoroh Tagame manga,

because then, I'll finally have
the body I want, a bear body
that could find someone to
make it through the winters with.

Instead of ropes and gags,
we'll have a red string that
ties us up, cutting gently into
our muscles and tickling
our body hair as we sleep.

Bear Ghazal

I exited a cave and was finally ready to declare myself a bear, but the
question remains to figure out how to reveal to the world that I'm a bear.

Will I buy a motorcycle and a leather jacket, showing my bare chest
as I ride down the beltway, showing that I'm a "live fast, die young" bear?

Will I stand in front of my bathroom mirror, contorting my hands
to get the best post-shower selfie, showing that I'm a "thirst trap" bear?

Will I powder my hands as I grip free weights and go for several
more reps, showing that I'm a "sweaty, but glistening" bear?

Will I carefully manage my body hair to ensure it lays across my
pecs, that my beard isn't too uneven, showing I'm a "Brawny Man" bear?

Will I be any of these bears, despite the fact I'm fearful of motorcycles,
hate social media, don't work out, and am quite an unkempt bear?

Perhaps I'll go back into that cave and give myself a few more seasons of
hibernation before I come back out and once again declare myself a bear.

Perhaps before I do, I'll gather as much bear literature as I can
for late night studying and next year I'll emerge as an assured bear.

Morning Afternoon Evening Night

Every morning,
I find myself wondering who I will see in the mirror.
Will I love what I see,
or find something about myself to hate and obsess over?
The days where I love what I see
have been few and far between lately.
I sometimes look into the glass,
wondering how I ended up here,
looking the way I do.

Every afternoon,
I tell myself that I'm going to love what I see in the mirror
and some days,
I am able to actually feel a light going off within me
and I have hopes that it will light my way.
I go to get dressed,
choosing not to reflect that my waist size has grown.
I tell myself that size doesn't matter,
that I should embrace and love my body as it is.

Every evening,
I'm tired after a day of fighting against the inside voices,
the one telling me to love myself and the others
who utters every horrible thing that was uttered by men
from my past who have too much room in my head.
It surprises me each time that I can hear them so clearly:
"If you lost a few more pounds, you'd be beautiful. I can design a workout plan
    for you."
"How much weight have you been able to lose? You must hate to look at
    yourself."
"If you lost the fat and fixed your lazy eye, you'd have a shot of being good
    looking."

Every night,
before sleep takes me,

I have the same conversation with myself while I am brushing my teeth,
looking at myself in the mirror.
Everywhere I look there is something reinforcing the idea
that I should hate myself because I don't look like everyone else.
I know now that this is my superpower,
that being myself is a magic all my own and it's what make me so
     incredible.
At the end of every day,
I know that tomorrow will bring me another chance to love myself.

JAMIESON WOLF

Metamorphosis

After my diagnosis,
my boyfriend turned to me and said,
"You're a broken man now. No one else would want you, but I'll stay."
I believed him for a moment.
When I looked at myself in the mirror,
I saw a monster even though nothing
showed on the surface of my skin.
Soon, when I looked at myself in the mirror,
I saw the freakshow of a man
instead of the person that I was.
With each new day that I carried his belief for my own,
my body grew heavy, and I knew only hatred
for the thing that I saw in the mirror.
Eventually, his hatred of me showed
who he really was and his vision of me,
what he thought of my disease,
fell away so that I was revealed anew.
When I looked in the mirror again,
I didn't recognize myself.
Touching the glass,
I tried to think of who I had been
and what I had become.
I realized in the end that I was still becoming,
my wings were still growing.
I could feel the nubs pressing against
the skin of my shoulder blades,
wings ready to slip out of my skin
so that they could feel the air anew,
dreaming of places to fly within.

The Will of the Heart

After my world changed,
I wondered how I would find my way around
the world of men who,
in my experience,
didn't want me anyways.
How would I find my way when I didn't know how to find myself?
Before, I had been merely disabled,
now I carried a disease within my skin.
It lived within me like a spectre,
able to strike at will,
taking away control of my body.
Still, I knew that I needed love to heal
and I tried to find it in the company of other men.
I remember one man.
We met for a date, and I showed up with my cane.
He flapped his hand at it as if offended.
"What's that thing?"
I sighed inwardly and held up my third leg.
"This is called a cane," I told him. "They're the newest thing."
I hoped he would appreciate my attempt at humor.
Instead, he rolled his eyes and when he looked at me again,
I knew that his eyes didn't see me.
"How does it feel to be half a man?" he asked.
I went home and seethed into the trees,
lost within the shadow forest that marked my walls
and hid me from the light.
My cane, the symbol of what my life had become,
seemed to mock me from the corner of the room.
There was another man who was shocked
when I told him about my multiple sclerosis.
"You're on meds, right? You're cured?"
I tried to explain that there was no cure,
that the medication just managed the pain
and it halted the disease.
He let out a deep breath and looked at me with eyes

that showed no understanding.
"But you're on medication."
He looked offended that there was no cure,
as if it were somehow my fault.
"I can't be with someone who's going to die."
I didn't want to spend the time pointing out
that everyone dies eventually.
There were others afterwards,
each man more disappointing than the last.
I was alone one night when I realized a hard truth:
It was hard to love someone when I didn't love myself.
I knew that it would have to begin with me,
that the love I needed wouldn't come from other men
but from within myself.
The men that I was attracting,
or that I was attracted to,
needed to heal themselves, and I
would not be their nursemaid.
I stripped off all my clothes and made my way
to my full-length mirror.
Looking at my body, I had a moment of revulsion.
I took in the rolls and curves of my body,
the scars that marked it like a roadmap,
telling stories of my journey.
I saw each mark and blemish and I could feel
the spectre within me trying to rise toward the surface of skin
so that it too could be seen.
Rather than turn away from myself,
I did something which required all the strength I had.
Placing a hand on the mirror and looking at all of me,
I said three words: "I love you."
It was a small beginning, but even a beach
started from one grain of sand.
"I love you,"
I said again. I would keep saying these three words
until I knew that they were truth:
"I love you."

I Am a Bear

I am a bear,
able to defend what it mine
and what calls to my heart.
I draw comfort from the sunshine,
the whisper of the breeze
as it talks to the leaves
and the low murmur I can hear
that runs below the ground.
I am bear.
Drawing guidance from the stars,
I follow their paths across the sky
so that I may find others
that my spirit recognizes as home.
I look to the skies
and see the coming winter.
Those I love are warmth against the wind.
I bear.
When I become lost,
I simply look to the stars above me
so that they can guide me
to where I need to be.
I answer to the call of the trees
and the other animals of the forest
that know a language beyond words.
Bear,
I hold my spirit aloft
so that I may bare what is within,
letting the sunlight and the moon
shine down upon me.
I let go of my earthly body,
following my heart as it runs
with the wind.

Bellyache

When the first thing you do is to rub my stomach,
your hands eager to roam—
your lecherous partner watching—
you stop and squint. You reach into your bag,

start gently burnishing my stomach with Brasso,
hoping to see my chrome
skin permitting, the prize:
a wish that can make your desire true:

to remove everything except the stomach
which floats towards you,
looking like a teardrop
or an egg, right into your waiting arms.

When you start to tickle its bellybutton, there,
almost invisible,
the frame that holds it laughs,
is thrilled at the attention. In the right light,

it's a person but you have one more wish.
You lay your head on me.
I become your pillow.
Invisible guts leak onto the floor.

Tactics
after a misreading of a line by Brian Kirk

I am an insult managed,
held up to the light to see the joins
but he doesn't feel damaged—
I am an insult managed,
sexualized and held against the groin,
transformed to his advantage—
I am an insult managed,
his reply nonsensical, disjointed,
my words remain unexamined—
I am an insult imagined,
he smiles at me, our hands conjoint,
like nothing I could say would disappoint,
his love for me, pure, impassioned,
we embrace, ensuring that I miss the point.

MARK WARD

Matter

He wants our sex to be endless
hours without cumming but not
tantric. It feels like control: it's
not enough for him to fuck me,

he needs to catalogue my skin,
spread larger than his bored tautness.
*Why do fat guys never know how
much they weigh?* A checkmark left unimpressed.

I don't want to look at myself
in his mirrored double wardrobe
that fails to tame all the angles.

I'm better when self-directed.
I close my eyes and see my body
alone, thinner, beautiful, mid-twenties.

The Hotel Mirror

hides nothing.
All that laziness
I ate onto myself.
But still, it's not
that bad. I turn
to profile. My
stomach hangs
like a tear
drop. I can still
see my dick,
I haven't crossed
that line. Why
would anyone want to
fuck me? I've got
a good face but this
smock of a body, this
oversized comedy apron,
how did it happen? I know.
I ate the evening,
the fading light, the feeling
I should starve myself
or stay in the shower
until it fogs up the mirror
and I can forget.

MARK WARD

Heft

Those thin men, skeletons
in tight flesh. They say you've
    put on weight since
the whole "new clothes" affair—
but at least there's no more pretence.
    They were sure of your
shame, but instead you revelled
in how your body moved; let those
    knights aspire to tautness—
you installed mirrors, had seconds,
took to walking around the palace
    naked and gloriously feckless.

I had left home, being the youngest
and having eaten them out of it, I found
    a job as a footman; yours.
You liked to inspect us yourself
(which caused a whisper) when
    company was coming—
some queen and her stable of princesses
to dangle under your nose. That day,
    you wore a robe, just about.

My uniform didn't fit and I bulged
out of it, embarrassed. We didn't speak
    but a week later, one arrived,
tailor-made. The others noticed and
the first footman told me to go and
    say thank you.
At your room, the maid said you were
in the library. Asleep naked in a chair,
    your book had slid down, covering

nothing—you awoke and stared at me,
still half-asleep, before realizing your body

had woken too. You were embarrassed,
something no one had seen you be since
that day the whole town laughed at you,
    not for your body but your gullibility.
You had swooned over the tailor, you later told me,
his barrel-chest, his measuring tape covering every
    inch of you. You wanted it to be true.

Now, you reached for a robe and covered yourself,
abashed. *I'm sorry for interrupting, Sire.* And you
    laughed, smiled. *You didn't. Jones, isn't it?*
I instinctively straightened up. *Yes, Sire.* And you
didn't speak for a long minute. *I'm glad to see that
    your new attire suits you well. I wanted you
to be comfortable in it, a handsome man like yourself.*
The next day, dressed, you sat and spoke with me,
    about small things, palace life, everything.

Within a few weeks, our visits were twice daily.
You asked if I would be happy to spend my time with you
    as your personal footman. You stared at the ground,
nervous I would say no. *I'd really like that but there's
just one thing.* You sighed, regretting saying anything.
    The clothes you've been wearing have got to go.
You smiled but said, *I can't, not around you.* I undid your buttons,
your breeches and kissed you, embracing your heft. I stripped too
    and brought us to the mirror to see us in our finery.

JER LOUDENBACK

A Dense Dream

Another long Minnesota winter
has finally come to a halt.
Feeling the warm air coming into his den,
a bear wakes up slowly from his hibernation …

Alas, how the dense forest shimmers
from the long snowy weight gone!
The smell of wet musk and pine trees rises from the floor
Among the tall trees and new plants springing.

As he slowly walks, his paws can feel
The softness of earth pushing back.
He stands up on his hind legs,
Snorting up at the sky and taking a deep breath.

A wave of euphoria hits him
As he walks to a tall tree with its rough bark.
He embraces the tree, his claws scratching.
It feels happily forever.

Yet he soon feels someone scratching his back.
He doesn't feel scared. Just a bit puzzled.
Closing his eyes, he slides to the ground,
Frotting and rolling around and sniffing …

The grass in his nose feels strangely familiar.
He awakens to realize that he's a human
Atop his furry partner in bed. He closes his eyes,
Allowing the dense fur to sigh into his nose.

An Otter Gathering

Some years ago, I was invited to an Otter pool party.
"What is an Otter?" I said.
My friend said, "Oh, you haven't heard? It's a new name
For hairy men who are lean unlike Bears."
I was intrigued. I didn't know I was a type in the Bear community.

On the day of the party, I wandered into my closet
Looking for an ideal outfit. What to wear?
It took me nearly forever in the closet (no pun indeed!).
I ended up with a striped tank top (to show off my tattoo and shoulder
    hair!)
And simple shorts with 4 inches inseam (of course, giving a good glimpse
    of my basket)
With my brown Speedos (don't ask me why—you know what this is for!).
Facing the mirror, I hoped I looked dashing enough.

On my way to the pool, I imagined what the party would look like,
Men chatting with their drinks in their hands.
What topics would they discuss?
Or would they romp about in groups?
You see, I am Deaf and not of the "Can you read my lips?" kind.
Of course, all that would be hard for me
To follow spoken conversations.

When I met the host, he knew some sign language
To my happy surprise. I suddenly felt welcome.
The backyard had a nice number of Otters.
The host introduced me to few of them.
As I expected, some of them felt awkward about my communication style.
Nonetheless, the host made an announcement which I couldn't follow.

Then he turned to me and signed,
"I've asked them not to use voices for the next hour."
Some of them came to me and stripped off my clothes
Leaving my Speedos intact.

To my surprise, they also grabbed me by the arms
And threw me in the pool!
Then they all jumped in too!
We started playing together without our voices.
I was in heaven in such a bevy of merry Otters.

Overlooked

On a gorgeous sunny Sunday morning,
I was supposed to go out for a brunch get-together.
I arrived early at the restaurant
so I thought to walk some blocks to kill the time.
Everything around me looked pretty much the same.
Behold! A sexy guy walked toward me on the sidewalk.
He was bearish-looking with nice tufts of hair poking out of his collar.
And OMG! Those wiry hairy arms!
I could caress them and nibble every piece of his fur!
Best of all, he was wearing shorts,
Showing off thick hairs on his legs!
It was enough to make me drool instantly.
As we approached to pass each other,
we nodded at the same time. How strange!
I felt a deep sigh after we passed.
He had to be just another hearing guy
Who didn't know anything about Deaf culture.
At the end of the block, I happened to turn
on my way back to the restaurant. Guess what?
In the distance the bearish guy was signing
With my friend. How I laughed!
I hurried toward them and introduced myself
In ASL: "Hello! Not realize you Deaf same-me!
Very happy meet-you!" He laughed.
"Me think you hearing same.
Sorry overlook you." It was so nice
Not to stress about communicating fully and clearly.
This time I didn't feel overlooked.

JER LOUDENBACK

Seeing Paul Bunyan Up Close

A group of polar bears stopped off a tour bus
At the statue of Paul Bunyan and his ox sidekick Babe.
As the tour guide was about to explain the famous statue,
One guy said, "Look at that strange bulge!"
Another said, "Yeah, imagine if we switched Gulliver with Paul Bunyan."
A short guy said, "Imagine Paul being tied down with all the little bears all
    over him."
Then someone said, "Imagine how he'd look naked!"
"Oh, what if Paul got hard?"
"Just how are we going to deal with his huge cock?"
"Worship it. What else?"
"The smell of his sweat would be so intoxicating!"
"We could jump on those nips like a trampoline until they get springy!"
"Or ride all over his roller coaster tongue!"
"Or climb up his veiny shaft!"
"Can you imagine getting lost in the gnarly dense woods in his pubes?"
"Oh, you know what'd be even better? Go spelunking in the mossy cave
    underneath."
"Know what'd be even more fun? Dive into the cum pool inside his belly
    button!"
The tour guide's eyes jolted wide awake from hearing all this.
Now he had to try hiding his own bulge!

Gingers

Long ago when I was a little boy
Growing up in the Pacific Northwest,
I always went to the beach to explore.
My favorite part of the beach
Were the tide pools, puddles of water
trapped inside groups of rocks
after the tide left the shore.
Whatever was stuck in these pools
Had to wait for the next tide
To come in and lift them away.
The tide pools had many animals
In them, but they were usually filled
with purple starfish. I always sought
out the few orange starfish. Their color
jumped out so easily in a sea of purple.

Many years later as an adult, I went
Out to the bars. A few of them were
In the basement. I remember this one time
Where I was going down the stairs
And I immediately thought of the tide pools:
Before me was a sea of many men
Talking, dancing, drinking all over
In the dimness. Their brown and black hair
Were a bit hard to discern, but the colors
Of ginger hair—red to orange to blond—
Jumped out at me. I recalled how
I touched these bright orange starfish,
Feeling their rough texture,
And how some ginger men's hair
Could feel thick and rough, too.

M. J. ARCANGELINI

The New Neighbor

From the bulky pick-up truck he
moved through the rain toward me,
reaching out a hand in greeting,
his grip firm, but not hardened.
Pleasing features around blue eyes
slightly shaded by his cap visor.
Dark stubble reaching up his cheeks,
above the border of his thick beard,
and down his neck to where hair
curls out of his T-shirt collar,
promises expanding down his thick
body to its quivering, hidden root.

As we stood in the gentle rain
it was nearly impossible not to
admire him, not to stare, or drop
to my knees in the mud before
him to make an offering to his
beauty, the grace of his face,
the bulge I could almost detect
under layers of winter clothes,
waiting for me, inviting me
beneath his moist dungarees.

Instead, I drew in a breath,
reined my desire and we began
to speak the unpleasant business
which had brought him to my yard.
His beauty will fade from my mind
as he becomes no more than an
agent of unwelcome change, killer
of my beloved orchard, a dreaded
future arriving much too soon.

Repeat Performance

On a dirty mattress in the
back of a musty camper
smelling of mildew and musk,
sitting on flat tires amid a clutch
of other derelict vehicles in
a cluttered, maze-like yard,
on a gritty hot night
cruelly lit by streetlight,
we both stripped
down to socks and
he presented his body
to me for the second time.
We'd first met through an app
a couple of weeks previously.
Now here he was again with
that beautiful hairy ass
back in the air for me,
belly hanging down
so I could revisit the lush fur
growing there as I
fucked him.
But something wasn't quite right.
His was the same
round, furry body which
so excited me last time.
Mine was the same hungry
cock thrusting in and out,
but it wasn't working for me
and I could tell it wasn't
working for him either. Nobody came.
I rendered a bored thank you,
dressed and left him
curled up, naked and alone,
waiting for something
which wasn't going to happen.

M. J. ARCANGELINI

Walt Whitman Attends a Gay Pride Parade (2015)

The Bears asked Whitman to march with them
in the great San Francisco Pride Parade held two days
after the Supreme Court legalized same-sex marriage.
They put him in a convertible with the top down,
bedecked with the brown, white and black striped flags
they have adopted as theirs, a bear paw print in one corner.
He rode on the top of the back seat, high, where he could be seen.
Flannel, denim, and leather clad bears walking along side,
acolytes, an honor guard who all respected who he was
even if they had never read a word of his work.
Peter Doyle rode below him on the back seat,
sitting between the master's booted feet, ready,
as always, to tend to the bard's every need.
As the parade slowly made its way up Market Street
Whitman waved to the passing throng, a big grin
shone out from within the famous beard, as he
accepted the excited adulation he knew was his due.
All but unbelieving that these men lining the way
loved other men and the women loved other women
and none wore the mantle of shame he'd come to expect
among those of his own time, not in this crowd.
By the time they reached the end of the route
Whitman had proposed to Doyle, who accepted.
The marriage would, of course, be open.

Dasypygal

In the showers at the gym
after my workout, I found
one other man washing up.
He stood with his back to me
sensuously soaping himself. He
looked to be on the young end of
middle-aged, stocky build with a
callipygian ass, full, fleshy and
covered with dark curly hair
which, wet as it was, clung to
his skin as though painted,
emphasizing each line, curve
and dimple.

I wanted to stick my face
between those beautiful
furry hemispheres.

Then he abruptly turned around,
as though he felt my eyes on him.
I barely had time to look away.
When I dared sneak another peek
He was rinsing off. I caught a fleeting
glance at the impressive soft dick
poking out of his dense bush.
Then he was gone.
How I still ache to taste him.

His Hair

covers his body like a Persian rug,
like a mink's coat, an ermine's, a fox's.
Like the way my tongue wants to
cover him, circling his nipples and
arcing out to take in his whole chest
—if only I could take his whole chest
into my mouth at once, caress it with
my tongue and down to his round
belly, the hair so full, long, and soft,
then further down to where it gathers
thickest between his legs.

I lay myself before his body.
He stands next to the bed,
takes off his flannel shirt and
pauses in the pale starlight
before dropping his pants
and right then, before I can
touch him, before I can begin to
lick his cock and balls, I will
bring his whole body through
my eyes, holding it within me.

I look up, his hair tufts and
swirls over each broad, back-lit
shoulder like an alley cat spinning on
the crest of an ivy covered brick wall.

A thin line of bare flesh lies low
along his neck, a chalk line,
a scar, a border separating,
ever so sparingly, what wants
to be beard from what doesn't.

Atop his head he has shaved

designs in the burr-cut hair,
divisions, lines that change each
time I see him—the front so short
today while the back reaches long,
down between the shoulder blades,
where it blends in, disappears
like roots into the earth.

He turns and the hair is fanned
out across his back, a Rorschach
making me think of things
I can never articulate, drawing
desire out of me like a well-planted
and unavoidable question. It grows,
his hair, like wings! Like butterfly's
wings! Angel's wings! Devil's wings.
Then tapers shorter, narrower, fainter
sparser to the small of his back.
A dense patch rides that mound
just above the crack of his ass.

From there his hair whispers across
the firm and ample globes of his ass,
such sweet patterns, and slips gentle
to encircle his legs, furry and
discrete, to his nearly hairless feet.

Resurrection and the Little Death

The true harbinger of spring
        in these parts
The animal symbol of rebirth and fertility
        is not an Easter Bunny

Burly, friendly, open-handed
The Easter Bear comes bearing gifts
Sprinkling his bounteous seed
        on the ground
        and wherever else
        it shoots

The Easter Bear says
        it should be called Resur-erection
I stroke a luxurious pelt
Damp from honeyed tongue
        tease a naked teat
        Heretic, I say.

What? The Easter Bunny
        with his stupid candy eggs?

Hairy-tick, I say
        discovering another nubble
        a smooth niblet
        crowned by coarse
        and silky curls

Hairy not heresy. The Easter
        Bear pleasure grunts
        the fertility symbol itself
        stirring
        in its nest of flesh

He hibernates daily and awakens

hungry, and thirsty
and both of us
all of us
are keen for the resurrection
or whatever on earth he wants
to call it.

GEORGE K. ILSLEY

Full

He beats his chest
      and Tarzan yodels
But that is not
      the best thing he does

He doesn't always shower
      when he should
But that is not
      the worst thing he does

He shaved out a Valentines heart
      in the center of his furry chest
But that is not
      the only thing he did

Touching his breast, he whispered
      this naked heart
      is my heart and your heart
And then he teared up

He is a handful
      and an armful
      two big arms-full

He fills me up and I wish
      there was more of him
      even though he is
      already
      more than enough

Glittering Garnish

The way sweeps of hair catches
        the light
        (my eyes)

I make him lie in the
        sun, sprawled bare naked
        or near naked
        clothed in light and natural fur

Well I don't *make* him
        exactly
        I encourage him
        the sun beaming
        whorls of hair like eddies
        in a flowing stream

He doesn't need much encouragement
        to sunbathe naked
        because he knows
        what will happen

A large water mammal
        a walrus or an elephant seal
        ashore for mating season
        beached on a king-sized bed

The pelt, felt, stroked, admired
        the glinting swirls
        the plush mounds garnish
        undulating persistent flesh
        the body beard a glittering aura
        the warm light kissing and cleansing
        shining up every fine filament

Big City Bears

(1)

Lumberjack shirt
    big beard
    belly
    jeans
    boots.

(2)

Shaved head
    bristly face, glasses
    maybe a moustache
    sleeveless plaid shirt
    bear boyfriend.

(3)

Dark hair
    nicknamed Goldilocks
    in a throuple
    with 3 bears
    not good at math.

(4)

Goes to the gym
    carries his weight well
    guys love to hug him
    almost unrecognizable
    in a suit.

(5)

Not a bear cub
    despite his age and size
    also—not a twink top
    nothing so outlandish
    simply a bear.

Jeremy

He twerks in the middle of the dance floor
In the nightclub of my mind.
The strap of his jock peeks past the waist line
Of his jeans.
Last night I watched it from a plate glass window
Dressed in a pair of powder-blue shorts.
He cleans up nice thanks to his new job as an ER nurse.
Can you believe it?
This sexy asshole of a redneck is sticking needles in people.
He couldn't come near me with a cotton ball and a bottle of alcohol
But that would mean I would lose the opportunity to play grab ass.
Check those cantaloupes for ripeness.
I've seen that new husband of his a few times at the bar.
Zachary something,
a mouse of a thing, quiet.
I saw their Facebook wedding photos.
Could you imagine purple suits with yellow trim?
The last guy said no to his proposal in a club full of mutual friends.
Poor Jeremy must have cried for days.
It was the only time I felt sorry for him,
Cute bubble butt broken hearted bad boy.
In my wildest imagination we are slow dancing under disco lights.
We are that annoying couple
Who loves like no one else matters.
We are holding hands in his F-150 during the drive home.

Mr. Masculine

Mr. Masculine.
Mr. Kink.
Mr. Mentor Daddy.
Mr. Bear Top.
Mr. Man of Condoms.
Mr. No Strings Attached.
Mr. Pup Handler.
Mr. Friend with Benefits.
Mr. Smooth.
Mr. Hairy.
Mr. I Thought I Would Give This a Try.
Mr. Toxic Masculinity.
Mr. Undetectable.
Mr. Introverted.
Mr. Significant Other.
Mr. I Prefer Younger Guys, but It's Not Written in Stone.
Mr. I Prefer European Men.
Mr. BBC.
Mr. Pudgy.
Mr. Easy Going.
Mr. Semi Chub.
Mr. Let's Go Private.
Mr. Do You Cam?
Mr. No Disrespect, but I'm Looking for No One Old Enough to Be My Dad.
Mr. I Love Everybody.
Mr. Primal.
Mr. Chubby Chaser.
Mr. Unlock for Me, I'll Unlock for You.
Mr. I'm Just an Average Guy.
Mr. Rope Bunny.
Mr. Master.
Mr. Sadist.
Mr. Two-Day Load.
Mr. I'm About to Explode.

Man-Boobs

My belly is bigger than his belly
These arms are wider than his arms
My face is rounder than his face
His man-boobs are too small to warrant
Being called man-boobs
But they're coming in nicely
Friends at the bar like to grab mine
As if their triple meat cheese burgers
Sitting on my chest
I joke when I say
I'm going to have them removed
Yet when I stand shirtless
In front of my bathroom mirror
And see them staring back at me
Like two lumps of deli bologna
I contemplate more and more
About having surgery.

When My Mother Asks, "Are You Taking Your Daddy Out for Father's Day?"

"No," I'll say.
I hate how she switches on and off with my father
Like some light with bad wiring.
Monday she was in tears going on about how nasty he is to her.
I try so hard to get along with him.
I could hear the tears in her voice
She was trying desperately to hold back.
My mother comes back after delivering my message.
He said why don't you want to go?
My father loves to talk around me.
It's where my sister gets it from
My father is not the sentimental type.
He doesn't care about birthdays,
Father's Days,
Carving turkeys or dressing Christmas trees
With tensile and ropes of lights.
He said nothing the day I turned 50.
No hugs, half hugs or even a handshake or a knuckle bump.
I will tell my mother about the mothers who hold pictures of their sons in
    their laps and cry,
Of fathers who place roses at their son's headstones
On the same day they share with my own.
I will speak of being taken for granted like the coffee
Maker that sits on the floor in the food pantry,
Like the hotdog roller my sister sent, that's still cold from the Amazon
    Prime box it came in.
I'll ask him how two men can be in the same house
And yet it feels we're thousands of miles away.
How the sounds I make in the kitchen means walking in the opposite
    direction into a room of dark and cobweb.

Belly

You got a big stomach.
That's what a little girl said to me once.
She was being babysat by a friend of my mother.
I wasn't upset.
How could I be with someone that cute?
With a big sunshine smile?
Besides, she was right.
It's the result of my mother's cooking.
This is what late-night sausage taquitos will do
From a What-A-Burger drive-thru.
I try to hide it under tents of oversized shirts,
Behind hoodies and jackets,
But these college boys know.
I see how men with bodies better than mine cut their eyes.
My doctor prescribed *Ozempic*. It's 300 bucks I don't have.
Too rich for this prediabetic blood.
The stomach is hard to lose, my mother says
As she sits the baby back rack of ribs on the kitchen table.
I don't blame her for my belly.
To her I'm not invisible.
Not like I am in the eyes of others.

Mark

Friday night I'm going to ask Mark out,
Make sure I do it while I'm still sober
Before the beers and shots of whiskey get the better.
I'll conjure up the nerve somehow.
Take a deep breath,
Swallow my fear,
Dry my palms on my pants, and shoot my shot.
He likes men with soft skin,
Who feel feminine in his arms,
Who give candy kisses.
I'd like to think I fit the object of his affection.
The boys at school used to tell me I talk like a girl.
Who am I kidding?
Mark will probably say no.
Dress it up with flattery
Like most men do when it comes to me.
Or maybe he'll say yes.
I'll be fine either way.
Maybe he's the homegrown,
Cracker Barrel-loving Georgia boy I didn't know I needed.

BRANDON MEAD

Log Cabin, Rural Georgia

BEAR Magazine, 1991
Still glossy
some of the pages
stuck together.

Vintage like
the carved-out gloryhole
in the back room
of this dead club.

The personals section said:
Come build
a log cabin with me
in the woods of rural Georgia.
Come build
a life with me
where people will never know.

Three decades later
from this lonely barstool,
I want to believe
someone answered.

Year of the Otter

Re: Hairy trans guy looking to get plowed for the new year.
An hour drive to meet a married witch in an open relationship.
Full apothecary, distant fireworks.
He said, when the chants and spells don't work, he takes Viagra.

Grrr! I'm hosting.
While we fucked, I worried my car would get towed.
Full beard, hot furry belly.
He said next time he's going to cook me dinner.

Re: FTM in Charlottesville for the weekend.
I'm not horny, but I won't waste a king bed on a work trip.
Uncut dick, mind like a philosopher.
He said, for safety reasons, I'm lucky he's the one who answered my ad.

Woof! Door cracked at the Disney Sports Resort.
Donald Duck with a tennis racket like a pendulum above my head.
An actor, throated to the hilt.
He said, while I was sucking his dick, he totally forgot that I was trans.

DM: "All I Want to Do is Spank You."
I haven't even unpacked the boxes in this studio apartment.
Wide-palmed hands, sweaty from hitting me.
He said he'd get off later while he thought about me screaming.

Hi, Hi, Hi. Hi again. Hello. Hi.
It's just as bad as the first time I was here.
No talking, no chemistry.
He said he was surprised I answered, but no one is as surprised as me.

Grrr! You're so close to my hotel!
Left Body Paint Yoga to stretch for ten inches.
Stained pink on the sheets, blue in the shower.
He said they'd probably charge him for damage, but it was worth it.

BRANDON MEAD

Woof! Let me and my husband fill your holes.
Their fish tank was bigger than my kitchen.
Buck Angel on TV, mixed cum on my chest scars.
They said it was important to them to make sure I felt welcome.

Re: In Town for the Farming Convention
Back home he drives a tractor while his wife scrambles eggs.
Rugged face, cinnamon gum.
He said, a boy hole is a boy hole but mine is his favorite kind.

Alert: I've never seen a guy like you before.
He asked if he should wear leather gear or a business suit.
Cold whiskey, tongue on me all night.
He said I cured him. He's not afraid of boypussy anymore.

Re: Bath house downtown, room 204
This place feels like a haunted maze.
Heart racing, cardboard sheets.
He said, how the fuck do you make it taste like that?

Text: I'd like to see you again.
His apartment still looks like a dealership waiting room.
Bareback, dark indie folk.
He said he was glad I let him cook me dinner this time.

Woof! I think I know your boyfriend.
Maybe he doesn't remember that we've fucked before.
Bad tattoos, yells "Oy vey" when he cums.
He said he's not Jewish, just trying not to swear anymore.

Whisper: "I want to show you something."
Tonight was supposed to be a John Waters marathon.
"Cry-baby" in the background, smacking his balls hard.
He said he likes to go home soaked after guys piss on him.

Grrr! I bet you ride like a champ.
The employee tag on his counter is from NASA.
Beefcake porn, a sex wedge at the ready.
He said, welcome back, I think we went to the moon together.

DM: Your boyfriend doesn't have to know.
I told him we decided to keep things easy.
We have an agreement, but never talk about it.
He said, you're fucking dudes like it's your full-time job.

Alert: Bear Soup in the Desert!
Floating on a hot pink tube, I'm the only cat at the party.
All attention, one three-holed body.
They said, well, your hands are looking pretty empty.

Re: No names, no condoms.
Pants off at the door before walking upstairs.
Viking tattoos, a framed medical degree.
He said, if you catch something, message me, I have pills.

Text: We need to talk.
I didn't know I loved him until right now.
My car got towed, maybe I was cursed.
He said, it's been a great year, but I think it's over.

Full-Figured Mona Lisa

When he paints
I'm still as life
in oil on canvas
I'm smiling
when he whispers,
"Mon Salai."

When we kiss
I steal a glance
at forgotten eyebrows
I'm laughing
when he whispers,
"Mon Salai."

When we touch
I ask again
how we will protect our love
I'm crying
when he whispers,
"Mon Salai."

When he's done
I watch him sketch
Scrambling letters
I'm smirking
when he whispers,
"Mon Salai."

Not Looking to Dance

Disco balls spin different
in a country western bar.
Over a cheap pitcher
served without glasses,
I don't know why I came here.
Boots and light beer
denim and full-flavor cigarettes.
The music makes me nervous
but he's so handsome
in the shadow of a wide-brimmed hat.
Smirk below his mustache
asking if I remembered my bandana,
I'm no stranger to the hanky code,
it's just that here
too much color can be dangerous.
Like the rainbow flag branded
somewhere under these Levi's jeans,
I'm worried someone will see
when he takes my hand
and leads me to the floor.
Fingers near my back pockets
I'm supposed to make a choice.
Paisley fabric on the right means
Single and Ready for a Partner.
Left means Not Looking to Dance.
He's ready to slap leathers
and bring me home after,
but all I know is
he's the one I'd want
if I ever figure out the steps.

BEN McCLENDON

Solstice

I wait for you like the pause
between breaths, like brightening
new light filtered through forest
canopy. New mushrooms fist
leaves aside, and I hold you
close even from here
where greenhouse gasses warm
sea beds and hills, where intractable
scores of ancient species
navigate by starlight as always.
Your hand on my face unthreads
panic from my bones. Your skin
gives purpose to my need for touch.
My dust will someday echo
this connection, but now
I cannot feel the breeze.
I cannot feel your arms, scratch
of your beard on my cheek.
Storms and swelter press heavy
air into lungs aflame from running
to keep nightmares at bay. You know
I have no defense against
your absence, so for now
sweat soaks me through, brilliant
morning burns the forest
grown overnight from seed.
How long until you hold me
among the leaves, until winter
snows us in for a thousand years?

Agassiz Peak

Rock to rock we leapt
as the creek roared beneath, fallen logs
our footbridge, red maple, tawny oak,
fresh scent of rain still
effervescent. We climbed

mountains, two or twelve
mountains searching for something
still green and when we stopped
walking stationary clouds seemed
still to move. The sky turned

orange as the leaves. I remembered
gold leaves on dry grass, November
in the desert, Thanksgiving in the desert
where leaves departed only a month,
a stand of bamboo still green,

hollow space at the base
of his spine, open legs, flick
of tongue, arched spine.
Each night after aspens
golden toward frost, I check
for the exact moment of autumn

when we held each other close,
still shaking after we
put our pants back on, clouds still
appearing to roll over the peaks,
sunset spreading from the mountains.

BEN McCLENDON

Erosion

Right up to the edge, toes on the cusp
and gravity, so binary, doesn't care—
it's off or on, falling
or secure, no matter how far the drop.

Stop breathing,
the world blurs.
Stop speaking,
the world speaks.

If I had wings, the tips of pines
would still look sharp, branches
falling one by one
from the bottom up. River bends

and canyons take time, but the fall
would rush by. Don't worry;
I won't jump.
When he's close to me

it feels as though the wind
could hold me, and if I fell
I could only travel
up. Sure, his smile and his eyes

etcetera, but really it's how
when he's near, the heft
of all I carry lifts,
how the horizon widens,

how with nothing but a look
he carves valleys
through the center of me,
how stones soften at his touch.

How It Feels to Get Used to It

This afternoon a raven flew by
on a strong breeze, glided
up the current, dove
down among bones of trees
to coast suspended
where wind snapped
limbs to earth,
and this is where
pictures and maps
run out, where I
run out of words to explain
how a late freeze
blunts the harvest,
how flowers pale
as they shrivel,
why the rains never come.
If there were a way,
I would show you
how it feels to never know
the same sun will rise come morning
or if another, sinister star
will replace it.
I would hollow the world
like a balloon, pad you
so you never feel
the jolt,
the recurring dream
where I drive the car
over the edge, the deep
water, the car
filling, the car running
out of air, cabin
shrinking, the car
plunging to the bottom
when the windshield bursts.

BEN McCLENDON

Navigation Failure

Blow hard on embers. Blow hard
on sand. Recognition is stronger
than recall until one breath

loses. Somehow light still
filters through branches, leaves
lift on a breeze absent

moments before. Hold the door shut.
Storm clouds gather as we speak.
Were there candles, they would

gutter. We live in an electric age.
How can chips like eraser-tips
store all the works of Shakespeare?

Radioactive sunrises
blow fallout onto beaches, cesium dust
on forests stunted by lengthening droughts.

I took our photo beside a casket,
funny the time we had
no time to savor. I held you

as if hours were endless days
proceeding from fountains of wine.
Time seizes embers, washes sand

far from shore. There's more
to us than that, I'm sure, but I've lost
the door keys, car keys, the map

to our new home. There is no chip
to store a lifetime's memories. If I could
gather seconds in my pocket, I would light

electric the road to our apartment,
open the door you left unlocked for me
to settle beside you as you sleep.

KEVIN BERTOLERO

On Passing Taylor River Reservoir

Everything I see is still—
another scene from our last day

until all grows unwell & then
another Christmastime.

We holiday in separate states,
a bit of heat from the furnace

as I make my way through
another novel—two men

in Sofia   desire at once
humiliation   & shame

& what I admire is they're
honest. I am neither different

nor the same, only missing
so badly some communication

or your acknowledgment as
I drive past a frozen Taylor River

for the second time, all those boys
playing hockey out on the ice

& I think I see you. They have
what I want—in fellowship.

Do you remember when I took
your photo under Greenleaf Bridge?

How cold you were? How still
you stood?

At the Isabella Stewart Gardner Museum

You step aside for me to take a photo
of the courtyard garden, but I want you there
so as to remember how you look, as when
you stop before Sargent's watercolor—
two soldiers lying naked in the reeds—
how your face changes, as on the opposite wall
Zheng Bo's *Pteridophilia* plays on a loop,
a film in six chapters with six men making love
to a thicket of ferns. Everybody stops to watch.
Mothers and their children see the Taiwanese
men orgasm and then eat the ferns. *It's organic*,
you say, turning to me, daylight shining through
the solarium glass, makes you look sacred—holy
as with a silver crown, my little saint.

KEVIN BERTOLERO

Only Once

Shower first—
then cartoons
on the couch
as I consider
what we just did   [your sweetness]
& when you
explain kinestasis   [pretty much a moving poem]
I admire your
early wrinkles,
wonder how things
would be if you
were someone local   [how long I've known you]
—tracing the seam
of your boxers
makes you shudder,
put your head back   [& I'm on my back]
& pretty soon
I'll need to brush
the snow, drop you
seven blocks to home
on Emerson.

 OH YEAH A BEAR POETRY ANTHOLOGY

Leaving Logan Intl.

It's dark by the time we land
in Boston and collect our duffels.
You borrow my black hoodie
to keep you warm in February
forty degrees. *It even smells gay,*
you say feigning upset but smiling.
I like to think you'll wear it to bed
the way that I would if you'd have
had something to share—or maybe
I should tell you to keep it—if I weren't
so anxious to pull it from your car
on Monday morning, how it'll smell
like you and I can imagine all the ways
you've used it.

KEVIN BERTOLERO

5423 Northeast 22nd Terrace

But first it starts raining as we're halfway down
East Oakland Park on the way to Mickey's
& when we get there we're soaked & the old folks
inside are smoking their Newports which you say
reminds you of being back at home.
You tell me how you walked everywhere when you
studied abroad, how many late nights with that girl
in the streets of Barcelona. You meditate with
your watered-down whiskey sour & I can't get
you to articulate exactly what you're feeling
so we leave & catch a Lyft to Bokampers where
I meet an elderly gay man who thinks we're boyfriends,
who pays our tab before he leaves the bar, old
doctor with a new house down in Harbour Isles
& after you finish your beer, when I finish my
vodka soda we stumble to the bathroom. You
turn to me & say *bed*, so I call a Lyft & we
head home. After falling in the pool, I drag you
beneath the covers still kinda wet—how you thank me.
I pull off your purple tee & join you. You roll
onto me in half-sleep as if I am her, as if you're still
at the Hotel Duquesa de Cardona, pull my arm across
your chest & I can smell the humidity, the chlorine,
H&M cologne on your fresh burned skin, in your
little cowlick which you claim to hate yet I adore.

Some Other Summer

I enter you
    alone
as if I know
this
    & taste
your thigh
whole back
seat of car

/ open me to this
what is some other
kind of state

& all
that I feel
now is
someone
else.

eyes (damn!)

calendar bears
fuzzy flesh
luring postures
dears and dares
fire inside burns
from bedroom eyes
allure, torrid, riddle
you show me
slow static shock

posture purrs
skin bent, stretched
to scan surfaces
splayed on pool table
kicked back over armchair
surrounded by teddies
flat on the floor
straddling a park bench
ready to receive from below

so much mojo
makes it easy to lose myself
inside fast breath
captured above
eye-fuck the lens
those eyes—damn
objects enhance
your two best features
various stages of undress

amber brown, royal blue
emerald green, bubbling hazel
each color speaks fire
I see in your eyes
I take my own mental images

bear he once say

razor sharp eyes
pierce dark dungeon corners
    he knows what he wants
    when he sees it
under red light, he spots his feast
lays over a cage, leash in hand
    lock on to your gaze
    how deep it lives inside your mind
he hopes you want him to lick your scent
sweat and sweet and sultry
    he wants all your fun
    however long you want to give
curves everywhere you like
calves dangle behind him, above his body
    go on over, stab in the dark
    where all things slide through bars
heart made not sorry for who he is
now always close to fellow furry friends
    his eyes light up
    all the electric in you
His Daddy Bear's gruff voice
full of green light and hall pass
    what do you want to do
    where do you want to go
what he wants he wants Now
what you want you want Won
    lean in to his ear and spell
    what Magic lay out beyond these walls
        inside my Mind there is no Limit
        to where we can fly

ERIC FRANKLIN CROW

IBR Saturday at the Eagle Tavern

piggy back ride from a fun Grizzly
around the inside bar and then outside
hold on tight but it's okay to trust
piggy back ride from a fun Grizzly
we stop at a bench for a break
I rub his shoulders, nuzzle his neck
piggy back ride from a fun Grizzly
around the inside bar and then outside

It doesn't take long after getting my cup
for Bears and Cubs to cruise and play
a hug here, a pat on the butt there
It doesn't take long after getting my cup
Gray-wolf Link is great at making out
a twenty-minute kiss seems like two hours
It doesn't take long after getting my cup
for Bears and Cubs to cruise and play

He's a woofy Daddy Bear ahead of me
in line for a refill on his red cup
from the front range part of the forest
He's a woofy Daddy bear ahead of me
We pick up where I leave off
with Link in the make-out department
He's a woofy Daddy Bear ahead of me
in line for a refill on his red cup

All over the bar, inside and out
We kiss and play and grope
free to be as much as we want
All over the bar, inside and out
lips, necks, nipples nibbled on
layers of clothing fewer at the end
All over the bar, inside and out
We kiss and play and grope

"There's a Bear Hug on 14th St.
No IBR is complete without a trip.
I went last night; it was hopping."
There's a Bear Hug on 14th St.
"I've got plans to be a submissive top
and we might be too tuckered."
"There's a Bear Hug on 14th St.
No IBR is complete without a trip."

Two buzzed and very horny bears
fall into his room and onto his bed
both of us stripped down in seconds
Two buzzed and very horny bears
not even waiting for an empty room
he's on his back at a corner of the bed
Two buzzed and very horny bears
fall into his room and onto his bed

Whatever he wants, I just say "Yes, Sir!"
hard or soft strokes, all in or all out
the buzz lubes us up where ID doesn't reach
Whatever he wants, I just say "Yes, Sir!"
"Pump it in me, every drop inside!"
Makes me pound harder and harder
Whatever he wants, I just say "Yes, Sir!"
hard or soft strokes, all in or all out

"Just say the word, Sir, and I'm ready
to blow what's been in me four hours!"
"Keep pounding, but don't you dare cum!"
"Just say the word, Sir, and I'm ready
We lock eyes, blue on blue
becoming one thrusting, bucking body
"Just say the word, Sir, and I'm ready
to blow what's been in me four hours!"

Both ready to blow at the same time
at his signal, seed floods the room

ERIC FRANKLIN CROW

words stab in time to my thrusts
Both ready to blow at the same time
our sounds the same as dozens more
scattered through the host hotel
Both ready to blow at the same time
at his signal, seed floods the room

force of sex

how the body speaks
strength colliding
    each stroke connecting
    each push inside
    pure, driving spirit
       from his hips
before you know it
pouring, pounding
    writing a code
    about heaven on earth
    however long it lasts
       back up into it
hundreds, thousands
of strokes, each a flash
    the best way
    to feel that force
    take it all in
look behind you
to all that waits you
    coming to you
    from the next space
       double-entendre dimension
    filled with techniques
    for cracking the Bear code of today
       how much does it cost
       to get to the back door?

GARY GARAFOLA

Muscle Bear

Once your skin gave way like floury dough and we couldn't have THAT,
The teasing in the hallways seared you, burned your forehead,
Gym class left you like the cheese, standing alone unpicked
But oh how you fought back, hours at the gym, days, years
Until you shone like burnished gold but hard as steel

Now you are the one who stands in judgment at the bar,
Such a big man laughing at the weaker specimens
The men you deem imperfect, clumsy,
Leaving them off of your team of similar simians,
Taunts which scar and shoulders that freeze and close out,
At last you became the bully who hurt you

Midcentury Modern

Curved spindly wood and garish shades of avocado
Who needs comfort when style is the key
Cheap paneled dens with carpets like raised hackles
We're mid-century modern to the core of our being

We stood for things believed in things and fought for our children of the
    prism
Who take up the fight for their generation,
We pass the torch but stand at the ready for whenever you need us again
But we'll take no guff and need no renovations

An Agony in Eight Fits (with Apologies to Lewis Carroll)

Is that White Rabbit flirting when he drops his gloves?

Why must eating or drinking change one's size?

Can I be Mabel if I feel like her?

And must a pool of tears always end with a Dodo?

Can the magic mushroom make you "bigger"
Or is this just more holistic bullshit?

A grin without a Cat can still eat Bats, but will the Raven like his writing
    desk
After his tea?

And wicked Queens still kill with a look but can be shamed into bitchy
    sheared Sheep,
Knit one purl two

In a forest soaked in black shadow will the bearded White Knight appear?
That last bit's just our fairytale I fear

Whip Me with Pearls

"You could whip me with pearls," said the voice outside the men's room
    stall
Me inside sitting
Where I fled from the dancing bear overload of the A House Bar
I hadn't been answering the call of nature
The call of nurture more like
Through a crack in the door I spied the speaker:
Black chained boots/leather chaps/jacket/bristling beard
You know, the works out of my league
"Whip me with a string of pearls," this time a whisper closer
"Isn't that a song from The Big Band Era?" I replied
My attempt at being tart
Boots squeaked as he turned a 180, stomping off
"Wanker!" he tossed over a shoulder assuredly wide
Perhaps he was right, inadequate at this etiquette
I was always missing a digit
Tired of reading the glorious walls of the stall I reentered the thrumping
    stroking bar
Here I spied Mr. Leather for real, dancing with a persona non wanker
Who had the required jewelry one assumed
No one spoke to me for the remaining night's duration
Conversation?
Clearly I need a toilet stall for that

Lavender Hour

Quentin Keystone took up space
So he ran from his home in tears
Traveling through the forest where the willows cried
He flew like Summer days over autumn leaves

He found a hut among the trees
A bookmark in the life of the woods and entered
Inside he found all the windows tinted in shades of lavender purple
He stayed until the sun slanted just so through this glass
So infused in lavender purple was the room

Delightful was his childlike glee
He soaked up the color like a sponge
He became unnamed
Unlabeled, free

Man Boobs

Your breasts developed at age fourteen
And clashed badly with your hairy chest and burgeoning beard,
You wore a baggy t-shirt to the beach and never let a soul get close,
In shame you paid the surgeon to suck them away
What was left was scar tissue concaved yet drooping,
Nipples no longer visible hidden in folds
One deformity traded for another you joked

Now at BearFest you see the free, proud and voluptuous man boobs
Touched, praised, and envied
You in your t-shirt once again
But back then how were you to know that the day would come
When your pre-surgery body would come into style

MARC FRAZIER

Evolution

when I was a child
you could see my ribs
through my skin
a skinny smiling boy
in black and white
photographs

the body something
separate something
to be made clean because
it had never been so

because that is what
I was taught
my father
scrubbing my genitals in
the bath as if there

was hope for redemption
as if you could forever delay
becoming a sexual being
a burden that meant

creating life in a married womb
abandoning all other joy

    *

at the age of fourteen
studying for an intro to physics
exam I fumbled with my erection
unsure if I were doing it
right

a new adam born
body new and alien
another version of
what it would become

growing hair in new places
changed my mind as well
going my own way
drawn to male energy
crushes on boy scout leaders
swim coaches teachers

*

by college a hairy bear
before the term was used
my first sex with a patchouli-scented man
who played guitar

after college a man
cruising men
the frantic coming to terms
with how sex and intimacy
relate or don't

always the return
to the body
for knowledge of the body
but the rest?

leather bars backrooms
the apps
sex with one or more
bathhouses after the bar closes

wearing clothes highlighting
my chest pelt my muscular hairy
legs signs of a real man

MARC FRAZIER

in days before men
trimmed shaved

*

as I grew older I grew larger
with different types of beards
and facial hair my body
a thicket for men to hug
explore
trap between fingers
smell feel

bear weeks weekends
pool parties
Bear Naked Club playrooms
the smell of poppers
and sweaty pits bears
who like it ripe nuzzle

the Growlr app
for bears and their
admirers
how much weight is enough
too much

I remember the development
of man photos
a series of hairy apes
evolving over time

what was it I wanted to become

Eviction Notice

I hereby declare:
If you're not LARGE
And hairy, do not call

Yourself a Bear.
Notice:
Chubs without hair

Are not bears, nor
Otters, nor those only
With beards but little to no hair

Or even a little chest hair
Bear chasers
Are normal and we

Can understand them!
But not voyeurs
Who come to our events

For a vicarious thrill
Like a mother bear
With her cub

We defend our territory
In gay nomenclature
So don't wave the bear flag

With its seven colored stripes
And bear pawprint
If you are not one of us for

It makes me angry if you do!

MARC FRAZIER

Brittanica Entry for Bear and a Bear's Response

omnivorous   carnivorous   We'll eat anything
herbivorous   bamboo   even you   when we smell
sleep much of   winter   you   beware   we'll be
can   move fast   on you in a fast   minute
hunting   done by smell   I may growl at you
growl at times   before me   in the sling
many   relish honey   my honey inside you
solitary except during   every season   mating season
     mating season   after breeding someone
male   no role   we walk   away
in raising   young   give us   a bear claw
cubs   emerge in spring   to eat   and we're happy
on occasion   fail   we need to   store fat
to accumulate enough   for all   those encouragers
fat to last throughout
winter
may die of starvation
once commonly in circus acts   all those   movies
pelts   most popular   with lovers   before fires
     bearskin rug   on a bearskin rug like
lack a clavicle but   a pelt on a man
have   penis   bone   an aphro   di siac
a short   stubby tail
jaws controlled at   jaws   powerful
hinge by a powerful set   trained to open   wide
of muscles   when in a bottom mood
     white   bear chasers
markings may occur on   crazy for white streaks
     chest   Grizzly   in a bear's   chest pelt
Cinnamon bear
curved claws   nonrectractile   claws out
Kodiak bear
     up to 1600 pounds   to stay out
Brown bears
     trained to move   can dance

rhythmically to music   as manically
dancing bears of   as any twink   wild
          carnivals and festivals   and sweaty
Polar bears   overwhelmingly   deep kissing   in
carnivorous   the shadows with another bearded bear
known to kill people   long enough to see   who survives

RANDALL IVEY

Abundance

Naked in a wheelchair,
I survey myself in morning mirror,
forlorn not at the presence
of so much hirsute flesh
but at the lack of a strong young lover
to celebrate the abundance
with quick tongue-flicks on pink nipples,
with slow jerking hand grown frantic
on an old man's triumphant cock.
When we grow old and fat,
we do not bury the capacity for love
in folds and wrinkles
but extend its possibilities
beyond the tired and the clichéd.

Hole

There is a hole in this heart shaped like you:
Six feet one and graceful of line.
Should you be of such mind,
or suddenly inclined to charity,
feel free to fold yourself into it.
You would fit just fine.

Super, Man

Sciatica-ridden and obese,
I could not move from the low-slung chair
in the Activities Center.
The students stared at me as if I
had invented hopeless immobility
and were a beached walrus to be merely ogled.
Not a one of them moved to help.
Only the center's young director
evinced any compassion.
She put out an APB for assistance.
"Call Burton," I said. "He'll come."
You were at Study Hall. I had just greeted you.
The woman went to fetch you.
I saw your grinning visage approach.
You wore a yellow hoodie and brown pajama bottoms.
a perfect costume for a modern-day super hero.
No doubt, I had interrupted your virtual homework
or, more likely, some TikTok binging.
"My Superman!" I said happily.
I took the hand you offered and you gently pulled.
I rose. "Look at this kid," I told the indifferent ones
around us, "Like lifting a leaf."
"Nothing to it," you replied and steadied me.
Then I had to let go of your hand.

Hitchcock

Fools for the fair-headed.
That is one connection, Master,
I can claim with you.
The others—not so glamorous:
Head steadily losing hair,
Belly quickly gaining girth.

It is our mechanism:
Piling pound upon pound
To make ourselves too grotesque
For the messy vagaries of intimacy;
A way selfishly to protect the
Isolation each poet needs,

Whether he writes in ink or celluloid.
Fantasy too is a shield against
Relations that end awkwardly
Or never begin at all.
It is, after all, easier to relate
To chocolate éclair than to man or woman.

That leaves make-believe,
The realm where beauty accepts beast
As though he were beauty himself
Even with hairless head and bulbous gut.
"Your beauty comes from the inside,"
Saintly pale shade is quick to tell us.

But then again we are not beasts
In dreams; we are Grant and Gavin,
Pitt and Clooney, all flaws fuzzed
Out by judicious eye of inner camera:
Heads sprouting, guts melting,
We make our stake in love.

Troublesome Tippi and Vera aloof.
My blond ideals spot names
Like Dane and Justin and Stuart
But are no less elusive than yours
And no less worthy of cinematic enshrinement
And hapless love.

More to Love

Forget the porn,
with its redundant ballet
of kiss-suck-rim-fuck.
Fantasize more freshly.
Consider the possibilities:
For instance, a broad belly
would make an excellent front
for frenzied frottage,
and man-tits a warm haven
for thrusting phallus.

ED MADDEN

A Theory of Adolescent Male Sexual Development

1 – introduction

A postcard photo of Tom Selleck (c. 1985).

2 – literature review, key sources

Grizzly Adams
James T. West
Adam Cartwright

Pete Cochran
Steve Austin
Magnum P. I.

David Hodo

3 – application of principles / examples

Junior high school PE coach.
Moustache. Tennis lessons. Wrestling.

High school bus driver.
Moustache. Shop class. Forearms.

Guy who worked on my dad's farm.
Moustache. Hairy chest and stomach.

Often took his shirt off in the summer.

4 – afterword, afterward

The peppery smell of your chest.

On the Social Construction of Taste

Remember when we went
to Nob Hill, spent
the day? You liked that
Fabio fellow, all
long hair and pecs,
who whipped his hair while
he straddled your lap
and sent my specs flying.
For me it was the fuzzy jock
wearing white tube socks,
with green stripes at the top.
Three socks.

ED MADDEN

Mr. Bear
Myrtle Beach, SC, May 2006

At the bear contest at the beach, the bar
was mostly full of white guys. Our old

neighbor, who'd said he once worked for Disney,
who'd been evicted, had reinvented himself

there among the bears. Another friend,
the one openly Republican gay in the state

pride organization, invited me to be
a judge for the contest. He said that bears

are about acceptance. Another man said bears
were a reaction to clones, to ageism and body

fascism—maybe drag queens, fairies, twinks.
Bears are about acceptance. Contestants

lined up at the front of the bar, displaying
hairy chests and body positivity. One

was in leather. One wore denim overalls,
one suspender undone and dangling. Another

was a bearded ginger. In the interviews earlier
in the day, I had asked about visibility and

advocacy on behalf of the larger community.
Only one bear from somewhere more rural

seemed hesitant. Later, at the hotel, there
was a meet-and-greet in someone's suite.

The music was loud. Little was said. I don't
remember how it was explained, some kind

of ritual. A line of lined-up men were single.
This was all before cellphones and apps,

just AOL on the laptop back in the room
if the wireless was working. My husband—

my *husbear* someone corrected me—was amused
but not aroused. That was me. I don't

remember who won. I think it was the big
librarian, though maybe it's just that he was

my favorite, he was *just right*. I remember
the bar, the rooms full of men, the dark suite,

the trappings of a fraternal organization
with its own traditions and recognitions,

the sense of not quite fitting in. My friend
said that bears are about acceptance.

ED MADDEN

My Husband Who is Not My Husband

His priestly gestures, consecrating the broken eggs,
hands moving over the stove, slabs of meat

skittering in grease, drop biscuits big as a cat's
head, threaded with cheese.

Him, making the fountain, making lantana, acanthus,
making bloom and ripple, song, making the birds.

My husband, the blue room, the bright room, best china,
best silver lifted from a box in the closet,

its red beds of best silver, put back later for later.
My husband who is not my husband who is still mine.

See him, crying in the Dublin airport—
he doesn't want you to see. Can you see

the eucomis, its waxy leaves, its stalk blossoming
in the hot sun, pushing up among the marigolds?

Scars from this or that on shin or back, wrist or hand,
the way the garden loves him, the bees.

Him among the lilies, his hands lilies, his mouth
a twist of quince, his scent.

My husband among the lilies.

My husband, sauntering down the aisles. Him, sauntering
down the aisles at the flea market, dust settling

on everything, his small flashlight, his blue eyes,
his sound of geese, a train. Look,

something glitters and is gone. My husband, the gold
in the trees, falling, and him, a coverlet of mulch

across the beds, or asleep, the heat of him,
the hot water bottle of him, the cat purring at our feet.

My husband who is not my husband who is still mine.
The blue walls say so, the orchid deciding to bloom again.

JOHN FISCUS

My Cuddle Cub

Pic 1

Perfect smile,
Better beard,
Atop an actual mountain.
(He looks like an old flame I thought I loved. Actual panic WTF)

Pic 2

Green bowling ball instead of fig leaf,
Same smile but more smirk,
Naked bowling.
(Who knew? Panic shifts intrigue enters IYKYK)

Pic 3

Black jockstrap,
Assless chaps (ugly and necessary redundancy),
No smile, but get over here eyes.
(This boy is half my age, easier when you're 60 … he's nobody's Lolita
    … yet … here's my Daddy application let me know if you have any
    openings I could fill … LOL. JK. OMG)

Pic 4

Yet to be snapped:
Clothes or fig leaves or Adam before we fall?
Smile, smirk or snarl?
Alone or together?
(Maybe some moments are only meant to be so ethereal they must
    vanish. BRB)

Ele é duro e macio.

He is a mystery still,
I know
His lips
His curves
His soft spots
I know
Where he goes hard
Especially for me

He is a mystery still,
He wants
My lips,
My curves
My soft spots
He wants
Where he has made me hard
And he wants to know my mind

We are still a mystery,
He is there,
I am here,
We are united only in wish
Only in hope
Only in our cyber love
We are still a mystery,
We together are hard
And soft
And connected
And apart ...
We are still a mystery
Somos duros e macios.

JOHN FISCUS

Bigger City Blues

Some men
Have curves too.
Hirsute honeys
Built like Pooh

Big belly boys
Who shimmy and shake.
Big butts
My tastier cake.

Cigar daddies
Chaps on tight
Jock straps hiding
Their candy's sight.

Cubby Behrs
Smooth to touch
Rubbing their softness
Can be too much.

Suburban dad bods
A current fad
I sampled one years ago
Who wasn't half bad

Belly up to the bar boys
Come strut your stuff
It's time to play
Chose tender to rough

So many men
From plump to grand
A buffet of treats
To take in hand.

Some men
have curves too
Bring them all here
I know exactly what to do ...

JOHN FISCUS

Naked Bowling with Adam

He glides
Releases
Ball flies
Pin scatters

His fucking strut back
He smiles
Tightens
Balls shift
Heart flutters

Knowing his grip
He winks

Burly Muse

His
Single
Singlet
Signals
Surrender
Pinned
Plundered
Placated
Panting
Moaned
Merged
Melted
Marked
His

RAYMOND LUCZAK

Nap: 1988

After making love

for a scary fifteen

      minutes

my eyes close

      a sopor

on your lap

this humid afternoon

and my stubble

feels

the blips

of your pulse

in your Michelob belly

      sigh

while you

      watch *Creature Feature*

on TV with your hand

stroking

      my furry back

The Bully

Half a lifetime ago I was a tubby boy.
Snickers reverberated in my wake.
My name became a punchline.
The syrup of loneliness soaked deep.
Each morsel I ate was heavier than shame.
I longed for a kiss of sunlight.

Billy Grut knew the power of his 18-carat smile.
He epitomized the worst of wealth.
The barest shadow of his promises meant zero.
Yet he could snooker anyone into doing anything.
I loved him, and he fucking knew it.
Guys like me were good for a giggle or two.

It took me a long time to forget high school.
Yet the gay bars I attended echoed those years all over again.
My fat soul was a vat of 80 proof alcohol.
I lost whatever youth I had possessed.
I was humiliated when I begged God to save me.
In AA, I saw gay guys who'd hated themselves too.

I fought the mirror for the longest time.
I hated the curves of my fat: Was this really my body?
I didn't realize I was getting drunk on self-pity.
I needed a better education so I went off to business college.
After graduation, I treated myself to an expensive suit.
I felt unexpectedly powerful: a lion awakening.

My corporate ladder was full of appearances.
I learned how to tie my hundred-dollar silk ties just so.
I learned how to glance casually at my ten-months'-rent Rolex.
I learned how to trim my beard evenly on both sides of my face.
I learned how to walk confidently in my wingtips.
Then I learned how to make naked men grovel.

I had discovered a decrepit leather bar four blocks away.
Though I no longer drank, I had become the vodka equivalent of Daddy.
It was bewildering when gorgeous men begged me to dominate them.
I found their need for humiliation difficult to comprehend.
At first it was tough to call them names and order them around.
I didn't want to be another Billy Grut, but such power proved intoxicating.

My boyfriend is a former model who still works out.
He looks incredible no matter what he wears.
His fashionable friends do not understand why he's chosen me.
He says that I exude the musk of control.
He says he loves the way I fill out my suits.
When I have the need, I dress up just for him.

He says I'm the hottest man he knows.
I don't think I'm all that sexy.
I'm overweight by thirty pounds.
But yet how his face lights up when I unbutton and unzip myself!
Lost in the ecstasies of his tongue, I look down at his eyelidded bliss.
I've become the loving bully of his dreams.

The Mechanic

Can't say that I'm real book-smart.
Just a mechanic with heart.
Nobody knows I like guys.
Well, two buddies know, but I
don't go tooting rainbow horns.
Mostly I jack off to porn.

I fix stuff around my house.
Mostly I feel like a louse.
Guys online are so flaky.
Who'd want a fat guy like me?
Maybe I should trim my beard.
Shave it off? Nah. Just too weird.

I don't go much to the bars.
The city is way too far.
Besides, it's embarrassing
every time guys see my thing.
Yeah. I got a small dick. See?
Go ahead and laugh at me.

I wish I didn't care, but ...
yeah. I got a plumber's butt.
That's why I wear overalls.
So nothing slips when I haul
up car parts from the basement.
Then I sweep up the cement.

Maybe I'll fix a nice truck.
When I'm done, I'd kneel and suck
the driver's big dick and moan.
Maybe he'll get so blown
away that he won't care how
small I am. He'll go, *Oh, wow!*

RAYMOND LUCZAK

Learning How to Marry

Quietly, his eyes sing to me.

I flutter, a sparrow disbelieving his luck of finding
seeds cached by a forgetful squirrel.

I like how he towers above me: a bountiful tree
who has survived withering seasons.
His beard is full of tendrils that root in mine.

My life before was the Old Testament.
He is my New Testament.

Together we will write a new Bible
in which no one is more equal than another.

We will twin the language of trees together.

    *

In his eyes I am a changed man.

It is then I realize we've signed a marriage contract,
which has nothing to do with legalese.
Our bodies had shouted *I do I do I do* all morning.

He cannot stop kissing me on the lips,
fondling my spent cock and balls,
gliding his *ILY* handshape all over
the furry grasslands of my body.

He sashes me with pearls of his cum.

Sometimes a bed is all the kingdom a man needs.

The Embrace

So yeah, I'm sixty-seven years old.
Hard to believe that I've made it this far.
My beard dye job is ridiculous.
I can't get hard like I used to.
Sure, I can cum, but it's nothing like before.
I still watch some porn out of habit.
So I don't make any effort to ask anyone out.
Who'd want damaged goods like me?
By this point I'm non-returnable.
My baggage weighs a lot more than me.
So don't worry if you're not for me.
You already are.
You're probably thinking, *Is he bat-shit crazy?*
I don't care if you're twenty-three or eighty-two.
Doesn't bother me any at all.
I can tell you're in recovery, struggling to quit.
The scared look in your eyes is unmistakable.
You must've had to deal with a lot of shit.
Come right here.
Let me be your daddy.
Who cares if we're a few years apart?
Even daddies need daddies.
Let me take good care of you.
No, I don't want your money.
I don't care about any of that stuff.
But you know what I really want from you?
Your terrible loneliness.
It means you've had to understand some ugly things.
I want to squeeze that loneliness out of you
so that the only thing left between us is pure beauty.

I Can Host Tonight

I'm not asking for a ring for my hand
I can't have you thinking that I don't understand
I won't think you owe me anything more than anyone else you'd call a
    friend
Even if it never happens again

But I can't find what I need right now anywhere else
I wish my taste was satisfied by something off my own shelf
Yeah, I know you can't take me home but I need to get you alone
So I let my guard down

And you won't find what you need right now anywhere else
Such a risk in even asking but I'm trying to make us honest with
    ourselves
I'm addicted to the fantasy of having your naked body on top of me
Will you let your guard down?

Maybe I can host tonight
Kinda think it's feeling right
I don't wanna feel this tight
Help each other feel alright
I need to shake the fight or flight
A little darkness brings the light
We don't need to shatter heights

Yeah buddy, I can host tonight

Let's Take the Summer

Sincere
Cape Fear
Came so clear
Bad idea

Wide nets
Lost bets
Turbojets
Cricks in necks

Headphones
Pinecones
Missing bones
Dial tones

We're gonna settle this one way or another
We can keep the party goin' or make this a bummer
We're gonna settle this one way or the other
But I'm in no rush, let's take the summer

Top tier
In gear
Smear the queer
Recycled beer

Palm sweat
Eyes met
Stage is set
Don't fret yet

Cards shown
Claws honed
Blood and stone
Whores will moan

CACTICUB

We're gonna settle this one way or another
We can keep the party goin' or make this a bummer
We're gonna settle this one way or the other
Or maybe a third way, latex and rubber
We're gonna settle this one way or another
But I'm in no rush, let's take the summer

Latex and rubber
Chokeholds and hummers
We can fuck and fight all summer

Any More (66.67%)

I wish I was sure we should be doing this anymore
I wish I was sure we should be doing this anymore
I wish I was sure we should still be doing this shit anymore

Any more it feels like we only love 66.67% of each other
I just hover and wait for the next thing to handle and tackle and grapple
While my Adam's apple feels stuck and my chest tightens up
Any more my luck is crap when I'm brightening up
When my coaster hits apex and I'm raising a cup
Just to have it slapped outta my hand and the lonely brew is wasted
    soaking my chest
Which is still tight as fuck by the way
Calling it now, I die of a heart attack like my granddad did
Any day now …

Any more it feels like we only love 66.67% of each other
Less like lovers and more like brothers feuding, mothers stewing
Martyrs on their crosses and subordinates wishing for other bosses
Homeschooled kids with no basis or desire to socialize
Why leave the house when you already won your prize, but what about me?
I looped two into my dream and now I don't recognize it
It being the dream itself and the being I've become beside it
What I spend my time doing and which needs I've been screwing
Money and favor over intrinsic behavior
Bleed-out-the-ass miserable but keeping the status quo
An adventurer tied to two statues …

Any more it feels like we only love 66.67% of each other
Any less and I'd suggest we walk the fuck away
Maybe stay friends but take back ownership of our day-to-day
I could give up the malaise of my caretaker ways and work on my own shit
You could do yours if you had any of it
I'm so sick of saying sorry but I'm sorry you gotta hear this
'Cause I hear it up in here every day and hiding it probably makes a
    mockery of our partnership

CACTICUB

Which still feels right a lot of the time, I admit
I'm terrified thinking what'll happen when our lil' prince has to split

I love you but I'm not handling this well
I still love you but these quarters are feeling like a cell
I think I still love you but I'm getting too numb to tell
I love you but I'm not handling things well
Do we have any more? ...

Kuma Senryu, Vol. 1

Safe place to be shared
Cliques are quick to script a shtick
Safe if safe for all

Rinse away the grime
Clean contrast to be defiled
A fresh pig canvas

Reject fake fragrance
Pungent sweetness fills my soul
Sweat tastes like candy

Trading positions
From the top to the bottom
Smoke if you got 'em

Happy in flannel
Comfortable in a gown
Simultaneous

Just as we were born
Self-identity is key
Unlock and rebirth

Too thick for otter
Too thin to be called a bear
Who prints the label?

DANIEL EDWARD MOORE

Trinitarian Wolves

Like any threesome worth talking about
before the first shirt hits the floor and

after numbers dance their way into
a stranger's phone, you can always be

a little more reverent when it comes to
willingness thinking it has inability beat,

when it comes to desire's bullet train
blazing through your tunnel's graffiti

making it hard to read and breathe and
persuade the hand to rest briefly.

Over his mouth. Then my chest.
Wherever the lambs feel safe.

You Would Do Anything

Since pleasure's artifacts
remember the dreamers,
those who leave stains of
themselves on a world,
made perfect to serve
in the temple of empty
as love's leather boots
on hard myth floors
cradle the feet in
night's darkest hours.

In a room full of smoke
at the end of the world,
your soul is a mate,
addicted to beauty,
waiting for blue jeans
to walk through the door,
rugged visions from
the gym around three,
when the factory's
belts were burning.

What wouldn't you do
to sanctify sweat,
to give back the body
the praise it deserves?
Anything possible.

DANIEL EDWARD MOORE

Body Art

If his body was broken for half of you,
math can be gorgeous written in blood, but

when the dream ends that wasn't a dream,
it's miraculous how explanation sounds,

especially from lips convinced they're gifts
wise men left at Mary's feet as Joseph taught

Algebra hard as nails, the young Jewish lad
wore like stars on hands and feet like yours

but not mine. My skin chose ink to scratch
the surface, dressing the flesh from a lexicon

of impermanent silhouettes. Piercing requires
a signed form, written in blood and gorgeous.

Bedtime Story

To behold him worship calm
without lack of will to burn,

like a firefighter praying
that water is enough.

Knowing all the time
enough is always never.

Less ceremony and more sucking
said the Oyster to the King,

said the snow in black straws melting
precious little brain cells.

In the hands of perfect strangers
testing laws of oral power, you

won't remember being lost
between line breaks and the moon.

Until morning finds us breathless
on the bodies broken syntax.

Remember How Good It Feels to Be Good to Yourself

playing hide & seek
in the shadow of a question
to please come out wherever you are.

Sixty years later, old boy, new man,
as the theater's red velvet curtains rise
and breath becomes *Hi,* becomes *stranger's whip.*

The tongue prefers Pentecostal
when the airway's shut down by invading forces,
as foreplay's fighters scan the isles,

for someone to tell them how long it's been
since good held them down with feelings.
Memories cannot be destroyed

by a 12-gauge pump of denial,
as the rugged face sitting next to you
says *why don't we get disarmed.*

Light's Toxic Hymn of Pleasure

Something close and desperate was boiling with the hope
of a doomsday daddy who thought his cigar was a rocket of bliss,
and like history, darkness loves Spanish moss tempting your hair
to make a temple for the conqueror's robe, sweeping every fallen
    boot
as the moon teases leather toes with steps, they will not take. But
    still,
that's me, singing for you, light's toxic hymn of pleasure, branding
your name on the back of my throat, home to your wood's
lumberjack dream, swinging the tongue's blade of yes, tenderly,
as promised.

ALLEN SMITH

Summer Reunion

The Atlantic and Mediterranean
should be sunk
so I can be near him again,
intimate as within eyeshot
like I was ten years ago
when he was a lifeguard,
constantly on his cell,
that clam held up to his ear,
not even knowing then
the one who would become his wife,
not that I want to be his,
just for him to be mine again,
my lifeguard, that is,
each summer,
all other seasons be damned.

Hickory

The hickory is offended
to be referred to as a tree.
You don't even know my name,
so no nuts for you,
it might say
if words could be extracted
from its shaggy bark,
which is offended
to be called a hickory.
You don't even know which one I am,
it might tease,
like one of many nieces,
who might be grateful
I don't name which one. I want you to name me,
the shagbark hickory might say
if it could speak
some colorful language
besides leaves,
broadcasting green, then yellow
as the stripes on a bumblebee.
Does it say,
You're the one who stung me?

ALLEN SMITH

Family Time

He plays with his hair with a finger absentmindedly,
taking for granted it will always be there,
like his child and wife.

She's never there when he calls.
For her, it's as though I don't exist,
as I watch their three-year-old blow him a kiss,
me fighting the same impulse.

We have little to talk about,
me less verbal than his daughter.

He shares all he'd like to change in his life,
me wondering if that includes his wife,
though she doesn't make his list of strife—
boss, loss, living's high cost,
as I ride the wild waves of his hair,
that jet-black spray
I hope to play with some day.

Ballet Dancer

I'm a ballet dancer in a bear's body.
You might tell from my tiny eyes,
no plumper than a ballerina's,
noticing those who ignore this version of me,
the older, cello-shaped one.
So many into oboe torsos,
like mine was.
I'm no longer surprised mine is no wind instrument,
can still see things afresh,
as though bending my head back, back,
like a bow.

ALLEN SMITH

Tattoos

As if frightened of stripping bare,
he's gotten his arms tattoed,
back too,
like some graffitied wall.

My eyes would spray an imprint on him
if watching him worked that way,
but his body is safe from that,
just not my mind's wandering near him
so he'll clothe my insides,
staining himself on my brain indelibly,
painful to erase,
if I wanted to,
which I don't,
any more than he wants to get rid of his tattoos.

Photo Shoot

My sister keeps taking pictures of me.
She can't find the right angle,
the one of me 20 years younger,
30 pounds lighter.
She looks at each Polaroid,
as out of place now as her disappointment,
as she tries, tries again,
her worked-out body
eager to work mine out
like pounded-out dough
into some shape it isn't.
She's getting a good workout trying.
She tries a photo from here, from over there.
I'm getting a good workout too,
though less so, turning this way and that.
I feel like a kid who's fidgeting too much for family portraits,
ready to crawl out of the frame,
recall, to keep myself seated and smiling,
the men who've recently winked at me,
their eyelids snapping at me as I am,
all satisfied in one take.

CONTRIBUTORS

Shane Allison is a writer and artist living in Tallahassee, Florida. His new poetry collection *Turbulent* is out from Hysterical Books.

M. J. Arcangelini, b.1952, Pennsylvania, has been living in northern California since 1979. Began writing poetry at 11. Has published extensively in magazines and anthologies. Has done an array of things to keep a roof over his head, some embarrassing or illegal and none of them truly lucrative for long. He is currently attempting, unsuccessfully, to retire. He has six published collections, including *Pawning My Sins* (Luchador Press, 2022).

Kevin Bertolero is the founding editor of both Ghost City Press and *& Change*, a journal of gay poetry. He earned his MFA at New England College, and he is the author of *Love Poems* (Bottlecap Press, 2020), as well as *Forever in Transition: Queer Futurist Aesthetics in Gay Cinema* (Another New Calligraphy, 2021). His work has appeared in *The Cortland Review, Fourteen Poems, Post Road, Olney Mag, Malasaña*, and elsewhere. He lives in Portland, Maine. [kevinbertolero.net]

Cacticub is a multi-faceted queer musician, writer, and artist. His art is part of the continual healing process that comes from growing up in a stiflingly conservative environment. As a West Coast native and child of the 1980s, his work provides insight and perspective through a unique cultural and temporal lens, ranging from bitingly satirical to meditatively introspective. [cacticub.com]

Alex Carrigan (he/him) is an editor, poet, and critic from Alexandria, VA. He is the author of *Now Let's Get Brunch: A Collection of RuPaul's Drag Race Twitter Poetry* (Querencia Press, 2023) and *May All Our Pain Be Champagne: A Collection of Real Housewives Twitter Poetry* (Alien Buddha Press, 2022). [X: @carriganak and Online: carriganak.wordpress.com]

Eric Franklin Crow is currently celebrating thirty years as a writer/artist. He writes about Bear community antics, from the political to the kinky. He has self-published four books of poetry and has a social media/web presence called New Horizons For Fifty. He always thanks his mother for grounding him long enough to discover his gift.

John Fiscus is a cis white spiritual queer bear. At 61, he has found a new role, elder. He offers support and encourages others to step into their full selves. His poems are inspired by the intersections of experience and youthful enthusiasm. Among the inspiration points are cyber conversations, his mental health journey, and liking the label Daddy. As a lifetime poetry reader and admirer, he now dips an ursine toe into the waters.

Marc Frazier has published poetry in over a hundred literary journals. He's published memoir, fiction, essays, and reviews of poetry collections. Marc, the recipient of an Illinois Arts Council Award for poetry, has been nominated for a Pushcart Prize and two Best of the Nets. Author of four full-length poetry collections and a Fort Lauderdale, LGBTQ writer transplanted from Chicago, he is active on social media. [marcfrazierwrites.com]

Jack Fritscher, now 85, is founding San Francisco editor-in-chief of *Drummer*, writer and centerfold for *BEAR*, and 1970s lover of Robert Mapplethorpe. His twenty books include the Lammy Finalist *Some Dance to Remember: A Memoir-Novel of San Francisco: 1970-1982*. In 1981, he was the first editor to publish the word *Bear* on a magazine cover. His first poem, published 1957, began his sixty-seven-year career creating stories, articles, poems, and photographs for dozens of magazines while directing and shooting 150 bear and blue-collar videos for Palm Drive Video. Read his books free: JackFritscher.com.

Gary Garafola has been through all stages of the Otter/Bear continuum depending on the year or more importantly the season. He has written some very dark fiction, a children's book, and a play. He can be found at his home on Long Island, NY where he maintains a shrine to Robert Aickman and Joyce Carol Oates.

John Genest maintains his sanity as a senior administrative assistant by writing speculative fiction in his spare time. A Connecticut native, self-identified Big Bear and Wiccan Witch of the East, John has previously been published in anthologies from Bear Bones Books and Dreamspinner Press and is presently writing sequels to two self-published e-books of magical realism entitled *Bearly a Witch* and *The Coven of Arcas*.

Benjamin S. Grossberg's books of poetry include *My Husband Would* (University of Tampa, 2020), winner of the 2021 Connecticut Book Award, and *Sweet Core Orchard* (University of Tampa, 2009), winner of a Lambda Literary Award. His novel, *The Spring Before Obergefell* (University of Nebraska Press, 2024), won the 2023 AWP Award Series James Alan McPherson Prize. He is Director of Creative Writing at the University of Hartford.

CONTRIBUTORS

George K. Ilsley is the author of *The Home Stretch* (memoir), *ManBug* (novel), and *Random Acts of Hatred* (short stories). His poetry has been selected for journals and anthologies such as *Geist*, *EVENT*, *Lovejets: Queer Male Poets on 200 years of Walt Whitman*, and *Best Canadian Poetry 2021*. He was also fortunate enough to have won a poetry contest in Dawson City, Yukon, and was awarded an actual gold nugget.

Randall Ivey is a native South Carolinian who returned home to teach English at the local university. He has published seven books—three novels, three story collections, and a book for children—as well as more than two hundred poems, stories, essays, and reviews in venues in the U.S. and the U.K. He is currently at work on a new novel.

Jer Loudenback has been Deaf since birth and is a mix of both Otter and Bear. A Washington state native, he moved to Minnesota after retiring as an ASL instructor and teacher of the Deaf. He is actively involved in numerous Deaf organizations, which he enjoys immensely. He has performed ASL poems, but this anthology is the first time he'd written poems in English.

Raymond Luczak (Editor) is the author and editor of over 30 titles, including queer-oriented books such as *Flannelwood* (Red Hen Press), *Lunafly* (Gnashing Teeth), and *A Quiet Foghorn* (Gallaudet University Press). He previously edited *Yooper Poetry: On Experiencing Michigan's Upper Peninsula* (Modern History Press). His next poetry collection will be *Animals Out-There W-i-l-d: A Bestiary in English and ASL Gloss* (Unbound Edition Press). [raymondluczak.com]

Ed Madden is a professor of English at the University of South Carolina. He served as poet laureate (2015-2022) for the City of Columbia, SC. He is author of six books of poetry, most recently *A pooka in Arkansas*, selected for the Hilary Tham book prize. He is recipient of a Poet Laureate Fellowship from the Academy of American Poets and an artist residency at the Instituto Sacatar in Itaparica, Brazil.

Ben McClendon, a former full-time English professor, now works as an instructional designer for Arizona State University. He taught both high school and college-level English for 18 years and earned his PhD in Creative Writing in Poetry at the University of Tennessee in Knoxville. His poems have appeared in *Indiana Review*, *Redivider*, *Stirring*, *Zone 3*, and *Rattle*, among others. He lives in Phoenix, Arizona with his husband and two cats.

Brandon Mead is a Best of the Net-nominated bathtub writer, poet, and sugar cub who calls the Pacific Northwest home after living his whole Nomi Malone fantasy in Las Vegas, Nevada. An open mic host in Seattle, his work has appeared in journals such as *Taco Bell Quarterly*, *Vagabonds*, and *86 Logic*. Originally from the tropical south, he is the founder of Queer Bewks, Wayward Pansy Press, and writes trans-inclusive gay erotica under the semi-secret pen name Leo Sparx. [fiercestorytelling.com]

Kenney Mencher (Cover Artist) graduated from Lehman College of the City University of New York in 1991 with a bachelor's degree in art history. He earned a master's degree in art history from the University of California, Davis and a M.F.A. from the University of Cincinnati. He has taught at the University of Chicago and Texas A&M University and various schools in California. He was a tenured professor of art and art history at Ohlone College in Fremont from 1999 to 2016. Kenney left teaching in 2016 to pursue painting full time. [kenneymencher.com]

Daniel Edward Moore lives in Washington on Whidbey Island. His work is forthcoming in *The Meadow*, *The Chiron Review*, *Delta Poetry Review*, *Book of Matches*, *Impossible Archetype*, *Drunk Monkeys*, and *The Broadkill Review*. He is also an editor for *Rockvale Review*. His book *Waxing the Dents* is available from Brick Road Poetry Press.

Allen Smith's work has appeared in *Asheville Poetry Review*, *Broad River Review*, *The Gay & Lesbian Review*, *Lovejets: Queer Male Poets on 200 Years of Walt Whitman* (Squares & Rebels, 2019) and *My Diva: 65 Gay Men on the Women Who Inspire Them* (University of Wisconsin, 2009). A bilateral leg amputee, he has a chapbook, *Unfolding Maps* (Pudding House Publications, 2008), and lives with his husband in Alexandria, Virginia.

Mark Ward is the author of *Nightlight* (Salmon Poetry, 2023) and four chapbooks: *Circumference* (FLP, 2018), *Carcass* (7KP, 2020), *HIKE* (Bear Creek, 2022) and the interactive branching sonnet, *Faultlines* (voidspace, 2024). He edits *Impossible Archetype*, an international journal of LGBTQ+ poetry, now in its seventh year.

Jamieson Wolf is a number-one bestselling author—he likes to tell people that a lot—and writes in many different genres. Jamieson is also an accomplished artist and a Tarot reader. He lives in Ottawa, Ontario, Canada, with his husband Michael and their cat, Anakin, who they swear has Jedi powers. [jamiesonwolf.com]